Steven M. Avella

I Lift My Eyes to the Mountains :

A Brief History of the
Diocese of *Colorado Springs*

· ÉDITIONS DU SIGNE ·

Publisher:

Éditions du Signe

1, rue Alfred Kastler - Eckbolsheim

B.P. 94 – 67038 Strasbourg, Cedex 2, France

Tel: ++33 (03) 88 78 91 91

Fax: ++33 (03) 88 78 91 99

www.editionsdusigne.fr

email: info@editionsdusigne.fr

Publishing director: Christian Riehl

Director of publication: Joëlle Bernhard

Publishing assistant: Anne-Lise Hauchard

Authors: Steven M. Avella- Rosalia Scalia

© Text: Diocese of Colorado Springs, 2008

Layout: Éditions du Signe - 107796

Photoengraving : Éditions du Signe

Pictures: © John Glover

Acknowledgments

The author wishes to acknowledge the assistance he received from a number of people.

In Colorado Springs Fr. Mark Pranaitis, C. M., provided initial support and information about this project as well as a basic orientation to the pastoral center, its staff and its records. Fr. Mark also graciously loaned me his car for a day trip to the archives of the Archdiocese of Denver. Fr. Ricardo Cornonado-Arrascue, chancellor of the diocese, gave me unlimited access to the archives and provided a wonderful place for me to stay while doing research in Colorado Springs. Sister Joseph Marie Jacobsen, former archivist, gave me a work space in the well-organized archives and responded to my every request for materials. *Catholic Herald* editor Bill Howard, Esperanza Griffith and Donna Gaffney provided me with back issues of the diocesan newspaper and a number of photos. Former *Herald* editor Joanne Pearring generously shared information and photos from previous years. Everyone I met at the diocesan center was welcoming, courteous and supportive. Likewise, a visit to the archives of the Archdiocese of Denver produced important background information and some pictures. Archivist Karyl Klein could not have been more helpful. Briana Johnson at the *Denver Register* quickly replied to my request for photos. I had the same kind response from Amy Moorman of the Archdiocese of St. Louis, and Sister Diane Liston of the Benedictine Sisters at Benet Hill. Special thanks also to Bob Roller of the *Catholic News Service*.

A number of people read the text and delivered me from not a few errors. I am grateful to Bishops Richard Hanifen and Michael Sheridan for their contributions to this work and their care in reading it in draft form. Likewise, Mr. Robert Doerfler, Sr. Patricia McGreevy, OSB, Fr. Donald Dunn and Fr. John Slattery all read the text and offered important corrections and criticism. Mr. Bill Lyons, Director of School Planning and Development for the diocese, offered helpful comments.

Contents

Introduction 6

Chapter 1: The Protohistory of the
Diocese of Colorado Springs
....10

Chapter 2: The Southern Uicariate:
A Diocese in Embryo
....24

Chapter 3: Come Let Us Climb
the Mountain of the
Lord: The First Ten Years
(1984-1994) 36

Chapter 4: Growth and Transition
(1994-2002).......................62

Chapter 5: My Strength is Made Perfect
in Weakness: The Sheridan
Years (2002-   ) 70

Parishes: 84

Introduction

The Diocese of Colorado Springs (1984) is a newcomer to the Catholic jurisdictions of the American West. Many of those involved with its founding and early life are still very much alive as this account is being written. Hence, the following is not so much a "history" of the diocese as it is a tentative snapshot of developments thus far. However, as the Diocese of Colorado Springs celebrates its silver jubilee, a milestone many married couples and institutions use as a retrospective moment, even this short period can give us some perspective. Context provides one important lens on the way events have unfolded. Colorado Springs is a part of the greater American West, the state of Colorado and the worldwide Roman Catholic church.

Although the diocese is relatively new, the presence of the People of God and the institutions that support its existence go back to the origins of Christianity in Colorado. Catholicism is a "universal" religion, with a common creed, cult and code. And yet, it has demonstrated over the centuries a remarkable ability to adapt to the realities of geography, climate, demography and local culture. Colorado is very much part of the American West–variously located by many historians but by virtually all as including the majestic Rocky Mountains, which bisect the state. Historians who study religion in the American West are aware that the region has a religious geography as well as a physical one. Mormonism has flourished in Utah and Idaho. The presence of Roman Catholic missionaries from Spain significantly impacted parts of the Southwest and California. Protestant communities of Methodists, Baptists, Presbyterians and Jews have survived and even thrived in parts of the West. Asian religions have taken root near ports of immigration along the coast and elsewhere. Native religions still flourish in some parts of the West. In some sections, many people claim no religious affiliation at all and still others profess agnosticism and atheism.

Colorado has had a history of religious diversity, and a medley of religious faiths have settled in and created strong and visible identities for themselves. Colorado

Springs itself is today an "Evangelical Vatican" as it is the headquarters of at least seventy-five different evangelical organizations. Catholic life has developed within this geographic and social context. It has never been a dominant religious tradition as the church has in other parts of the world or even in other American communities. Developing Catholic identity has always had to take these realities into account.

Religion was not the primary motivating factor in the founding of the state of Colorado. Other enterprises and activities consumed the energies of the state's inhabitants. Before the advent of white settlers, native peoples lived, hunted, made war and died for generations in the area encompassed by the state's borders. Spanish explorers and other adventurers were among the first European Americans to penetrate the region. Fur trappers and explorers, miners, railroad entrepreneurs, health seekers and tourists followed. These newcomers displaced the native Indian populations and brought urban life and political, social and economic development. Colorado began its steady climb to statehood as a part of America's mining frontier, which brought thousands of settlers to the region. Linked by rail and the demand for its minerals and agricultural resources, Colorado became a state in 1876. Colorado is today the home of a number of important military installations. These economic priorities were key to state development and social stability.

The Diocese of Colorado Springs is also a part of the world-wide Catholic community. Catholicism's roots reach back to Jesus the Christ. Over the course of its fascinating and at times complex history it has evolved into a substantial religious, social and political institution of more than a billion people with branches all over the globe. Modern church history begins with the Reformation of the 16th century and extends down to our own time. The Catholic Church, which transferred its presence to the Americas, had to redefined its theological and hierarchical identity in response to militant Protestantism. Church leadership became increasingly centralized in Rome where its curial offices inspired, supported and directed missionaries. In the United States Catholic life reflected variations of Catholic identity brought by colonizing powers. Spain and its dominions impressed their religious life and culture on the lands directly south of Colorado. French missionary priests brought Gallic spirituality and practices that embodied the spiritual energies of the "eldest daughter of the church." Catholicism in the United States began under the leadership of genteel English gentry. It soon

■ *Our Lady of the Visitation, Elizabeth*

acquired an identity all its own as it experienced the challenges of a varied Catholic immigrant population and a system of government that insisted on separating government from religion.

American Catholicism came to maturity in the mid-19th century as papal leadership in Rome consolidated itself in a dynamic way to meet the challenges of "modernity." Direct Roman jurisdiction over many areas of church life created the uniformity in practice and identity that characterized an epoch of American Catholic life. Roman-trained bishops and clergy, a well-defined theological system (Neo-Scholasticism), a major codification of canon law (1917) and a very distinct and (at least in the United States) prosperous Catholic subculture were all emblems of this era, which stretched well into the middle of the 20th century.

A decisive shift came with the convocation of Vatican Council II between 1962-1965. The Council and its aftermath represented both continuity with the historic past and also some departures from former Catholic emphases and practices. New emphases of the Council included liturgical change, a renewed focus on the role and proper interpretation of sacred scripture, a broadened understanding of the church as a sacrament and a better defined sense of its relations with the modern world. Popes put aside the beehive shaped triple-tiara, a symbol of medieval papal supremacy, and stressed the importance of collegiality with their brother bishops and urged a revived sense of baptismal service on the part of the whole People of God. Clearly, a new era had begun. The Diocese of Colorado Springs evolved during the aftermath of Vatican II and manifested the strengths and weaknesses of Catholic life in this period of church history.

Church authorities and generous laity sponsored and sustained the missionary advance of Catholicism into the American West. The first clerics came to offer Mass to the scattered miners and farmers who populated the area. As Catholic numbers grew in Colorado–brought in by the economic development of the region–the improving organizational strength of the church led to the creation of intermediate ecclesiastical jurisdictions and finally a diocese in 1887, encompassing the entire state and headquartered in Denver. With the creation of the Diocese of Pueblo in 1941, the Diocese of Denver was raised to metropolitan status and became an archdiocese. Linked by bonds of faith, friendship, priestly associations and transportation to the Catholic center in Denver, the territories of the future Diocese of Colorado Springs grew under its jurisdiction.

Growth was inevitable. As is the case in every large diocese, the areas near the central administrative offices seemed to garner more attention than the outlying areas. It appeared to some that the Denver headquarters had little interest in the remote areas of the archdiocese. These distant areas received few visits from busy diocesan leaders, and coverage of their religious events in Catholic newspapers and periodicals was scant and perfunctory. As a result, Colorado Springs, long a thriving community between Denver and Pueblo, developed its own close-knit Catholic culture. By the 1960s and 1970s, the archbishops of Denver became anxious about the pastoral care of the southern part of the large Denver See, and plotted a new configuration of Catholic enterprises in the whole state.

In 1974, the man who is the mainspring of most of this history, the Reverend Richard Hanifen was ordained a bishop. In 1976 his superiors sent him to manage affairs in what was called the Southern Vicariate–a sub-unit of the larger archdiocesan system–taking up residence as the pastor of St. Mary's Church in Colorado Springs, where he helped bring about an improved and more attentive ministry. Although not at first entirely clear that this new vicariate would eventually become a diocese, by 1979 the remote preparations for its detachment from Denver were set in motion. Some raised doubts about the wisdom of creating a diocese out of an area that might not have enough priests or money to sustain basic ministries.

Ten years after Hanifen's elevation to the episcopate–and after countless meetings, much planning and assorted acts of tutelage by Denver Archbishop James V. Casey–the new diocese was announced on November 10, 1983 and formally "erected" on January 30, 1984. The Diocese of Colorado Springs began with some of its administrative apparatus already in place: a small central administration, functioning parishes, a modest but financially shaky Catholic school establishment, catechetical programs and resources, liturgical life and the annual celebrations of the Catholic temporal and sanctoral cycles. Bishop Hanifen himself traveled to the small communities of the diocese, which included not only the areas in the shadow of mountains, but also the flat plains near the Kansas border.

Bishop Hanifen's extroverted personality and his intimate knowledge of Colorado life and culture were critical factors in bringing the new jurisdiction together. He took time to win the confidence of his fellow priests–who at first regarded him as a Denver interloper–and to cultivate leadership among the talented religious women and laity who served in the diocese. Hanifen successfully negotiated the sometimes tense relations between Catholics and the powerful military figures in the area. He worked well with local religious leaders–not only friendly rabbis and mainline Protestants, but also the growing number of evangelicals some of whose members sometimes did not even regard Catholics as Christians. Bishop Hanifen spoke to everyone: evangelicals, the military, fellow clergy, religious women, charismatics and the farmers of Hugo and Limon, the miners in Leadville, as well as the suburbanites of northern Douglas County. While controversial decisions like the closing of a high school may have soured his relations with some, his presence and concern for not only his fellow Catholics but for the larger community assured Colorado Springs Catholics a place at the table in the socially and religiously complex region.

Not believing himself to be indispensable, Bishop Hanifen moved up the time of his retirement and asked for a coadjutor bishop. In 2002 Bishop Michael Sheridan, an auxiliary of the Archdiocese of St. Louis, arrived for his novitiate year of training for the Colorado Springs diocese. One year later, Bishop Sheridan assumed full control, and at this writing still guides the affairs of the burgeoning diocese, which has more than doubled in size since its foundation.

Bishops Hanifen and Sheridan, and the many who have assisted them, have faced the same problems as other American dioceses–growing and ethnically diverse Catholic populations, dwindling numbers of clergy and religious women, as well as the challenges posed by a sometimes militant Protestant culture and critical issues of social justice, war and peace. To those who live in the shadow of the majestic Rockies, the injunction of the psalmist to look to the mountains for help –to the place on high where God dwells– must be more than poetic imagery. The reply to the psalmist's question provides the reason for hope: My help is from the Lord, the maker of heaven and earth.

The Protohistory of the Diocese of
Colorado Springs

The official history of the Diocese of Colorado Springs dates from its formal erection by the Holy See on January 30, 1984 and the installation of Bishop Richard Hanifen as its bishop. However, long before Bishop Hanifen's enthronement, people believed, prayed and created religious systems in the region. The creation of the Catholic jurisdiction, nevertheless, provides a new perspective from which to discuss the faith and community within its ten counties before it became a diocese.

Early Colorado: Indians and Miners

Colorado Springs is in the America West. Western historians distinguish the West from the frontier for a purpose. The frontier, an ever shifting reality and hallowed in American myth, was always a place of conquest and development–an area where white European Americans created a civilization on "virgin land." But the West really is a region–a geographically varied but discrete location (although historians differ as to where it officially begins) where people thrived over the course of thousands of years. Colorado was part of the "mountain West". Before white settlers came and put down roots a medley of Indian peoples lived, worked, celebrated, mourned, warred and believed on the lands now occupied by others. Various Indian tribes–Utes, Kiowas and Cheyennes–largely dominated the Colorado region. These tribes made camp on the vast lands that they claimed, not as personal property but as their collective

■ *Cities grew rapidly in Colorado during mining rushes. 15th and Market in Denver (1865)*
© Thomas Noel Collection

patrimony, which the tribe needed for survival. They had their own languages, cultural practices and way of life. They fought amongst themselves in bitter wars that took many lives. They also engaged whites who gradually made their presence known and felt in the region and who moved aggressively to dominate the land as they did elsewhere in the United States. One of the worst clashes between Indians and whites, the Sand Creek Massacre of 1864, took place in Colorado. Eventually, the Utes, the Kiowas and the Cheyennes were all relocated to smaller areas in southwestern Colorado and Oklahoma.

European Americans soon came to dominate the future state of Colorado. Spanish-speaking adventurers and explorers also visited the lands on the periphery of their vast American empire. The New Mexico trade center of Santa Fe constituted a major northern hub of Hispanic settlement and a base for exploration. Southern Colorado was home to many Spanish speakers. When the United States purchased the region called "Louisiana" from France in 1803, a curious President Thomas Jefferson sent explorers into the wilderness to map out the extensive territory and to send home reports of what they saw and found. These reports, reprinted in newspapers and popular broadsides, spoke of the grandeur of the mountains and the verdant lands waiting for the plow of the sturdy yeoman farmer. President Jefferson dispatched Lieutenant Zebulon Pike in 1806 to explore and report on the area that would be Colorado. Pike lost his way but did manage to give his name to the peak, which is now the symbolic center of the Diocese of Colorado Springs. Mountain men–whose exploits in the wilderness are part of American lore–not only provided pelts that kept Americans in coats and hats for many years but also augmented maps and other reports of the region.

Interest in Colorado quickened not only because of the romantic stories of bucolic beauty, but also because of gold, industrial minerals, health and recreation. The discovery of gold in California in 1848-1849 set the stage for a series of mining rushes that saw various portions of the trans-Missouri West overrun by miners eager for quick pickings. Later, more labor intensive and expensive forms of industrial mining took the place of the "easy pickins" of the first mining boomers. Huge transfusions of capital from the East created major mining sites, requiring large labor pools that transformed

Colorado's economy and demographics. Most who tried mining, however, went bust or decided it was more lucrative to "mine the miners" than dig and tunnel themselves. Those who remained with the business often generated huge fortunes, some of which was shared with local churches. The mining industry's bouts with boom and bust contributed to both the stability and precariousness of life in Colorado from the mid-19th century to the present.

In July 1858, Argonauts sought gold in the waters of Cherry Creek, Ralston Creek and other streams. The easily discouraged left early, but thirteen stayed and eventually found the precious metal. Before long miners from all parts of the mountain West and northern New Mexico had come to the vicinity of Pike's Peak enticed by promises of huge nuggets. The real fortunes were made by those who capitalized on the people needing food, clothing, baths, recreation and other accouterments of civilized life. William H. Larimer, a city builder

■ Mining was an important part of Colorado's economy. The riches of the mines were often shared with religious institutions. Mogul Tunnel Entrance (1897)
© Thomas Noel Collection

and land speculator brought together inchoate communities along the southwest bank of Cherry Creek and housed miners. Towns popped up all along the Front Range. Some lasted only a short time. Others were destined to remain. New discoveries in the mountains and the presence of gold deposits in quartz stoked the gold rush and further swelled the area's transient and permanent populations. Colorado City (today Old Colorado City and part of the city of Colorado Springs) was founded in 1859 as a supply depot and launching point for those using the Ute Pass en route to the gold fields of South Park. As Denver and Auraria (virtually side-by-side) attracted increasing numbers and as better routes opened to the gold fields, Colorado City declined. On February 28, 1861, Congress declared Colorado a territory of the United States and established its current borders. In 1891 another gold strike–this time one embedded in ore–took place at Cripple Creek. This rush not only grew the infant Colorado City but spilled over to Colorado Springs boosting it by 1902 to a respectable 35,000 people–a virtual metropolis by the standards of Western cities in the late 19th and early 20th centuries.

The Puffing Billy: Railroads and Colorado's Evolution

Mining provided people and industry. Other developments ensured a growing presence in the northern part of the state. In 1861, Congress passed the long-delayed Transcontinental Railway Act that began the legendary race between the Union Pacific and Central Pacific railroads. Once this mammoth undertaking had been completed the United States entered a new phase of its ongoing transportation and communication revolutions. The railroad avoided the high passes of the Rockies in Colorado, chugging north through Cheyenne and western Wyoming before turning south. The Kansas Pacific Railroad built a spur to Denver, and William Palmer, a local entrepreneur, added another heading south from Denver to El Paso. The Denver and Rio Grande Railroad, which linked Colorado Springs with Denver, assured the former's success. This network, crisscrossing the eastern part of the state, connected local resources and industries with the larger national economy.

■ *Railroads brought prosperity and population to Colorado. Union Depot, Denver (1881)*
© Thomas Noel Collection

Union Depot Denver

Health Care and Tourism

Tourism and health care contributed as well to Colorado's future glory. El Paso County, founded in 1861, was a product of the mining rush, but even more so of the railroad. Colorado Springs was founded as a health-care resort and began as the brainchild of railroad entrepreneur William Palmer, who created the town in 1871 as a railroad terminus for his Denver and Rio Grande Railroad. His plan was to develop a community that would be scenic and salubrious, especially for those who suffered from respiratory ailments. He insisted that Colorado Springs be a refined, morally upright and genteel alternative to the rough and tumble of nearby Colorado City. He even managed to keep the city free of liquor until the end of Prohibition in 1933. Colorado Springs boasted itself as one of many sites in the West that could restore the health and happiness of the well-to-do and middle classes.

The city also welcomed Americans vacationing in the high altitudes of the Rockies. If Pikes Peak was a virtual "gold mountain" for early miners, it was also a site of unsurpassed beauty, especially to Midwesterners who lived in broad flat lands and Easterners whose mountain chains seemed like glorified hills compared to the majestic Rockies. The elegant Antlers Hotel, also built by Palmer, received a host of tourists, including English professor Katharine Lee Bates who composed *America the Beautiful* in 1893 after visiting the top of Pikes Peak. Among the benefactors of Cripple Creek was mogul Spencer Penrose, who made a fortune in Cripple Creek mining, and built the elegant Broadmoor Hotel situated at the foot of the mountains. The Garden of the Gods, a hauntingly beautiful set of rock formations, also drew curious visitors who rode burros and savored the wide open spaces of the American West. By 1872 Colorado Springs had a population of 800 and was typical of many "health-care cities" of the West—water treatments, hospitals, large streets and a quiet and unhurried urban life.

The West, and especially Colorado, had what nineteenth-century folk called a "salubrious" or health giving climate. The curative impact of local springs, such as those that bubbled to the surface in Manitou, the abundance of fresh air—thought at the time to be the best cure for tuberculosis—and the benefits of fluoridated water drew the chronically ill and infirm to Colorado Springs. Catholic hospitals and health-care institutions benefitted from this preoccupation with health.

Catholic Life is Born

In acknowledging the presence of Indian peoples on the land, it is important to remember that they too prayed, celebrated rites of passage, marked the seasons and invoked superhuman forces to assist them in the hunt, the battle and the quest for food. Christians did not bring religious beliefs or practices to Colorado, but rather replaced existing ones with their own beliefs, customs and laws.

Colorado, too, had a significant Hispanic population that migrated into the southern part of the state from New Mexico. Although not clearly associated with the future territory of Colorado Springs, nonetheless they contributed to yet another layer of the rich cultural and religious history of the Centennial State. Overlapping land grants brought Spanish-speaking settlers, shepherds and farmers who carried with them the seeds of their Catholic faith. Historians Carl Abbott, Stephen Leonard and Thomas Noel describe the activities of *Los Hermanos Penitentes* who migrated north to Colorado and established themselves as religious authorities— and were active throughout the 19th century.

Spanish-speaking Catholics in southern Colorado spearheaded the first Catholic "incursions." The church of Nuestra Senora de Guadalupe in Conejos received a resident pastor in 1858 and became the mother church for twenty-five missions. Handed over to the Jesuits in 1871, Guadalupe evolved into a thriving Catholic center with a convent, church and school.

The city of Denver, rapidly growing in the north, had originally been under the jurisdiction of the Vicar Apostolic of Kansas, Bishop John B. Miege, headquartered in Leavenworth. By 1860 Bishop Miege had visited the booming community as well as the thriving mining camps in Central City, South Park and Oro City. He offered the first Mass celebrated in Denver in a store. Bishop Miege eventually secured two blocks for a church from the Denver City Town Company on the outskirts of the town. Later, he convinced his Metropolitan in St. Louis, Peter Richard Kenrick, to transfer jurisdiction of the Denver area to Bishop Jean B. Lamy, headquartered in Santa Fe. Bishop Lamy sent his close associates Father (and future bishop) Joseph Projectus Machebeuf and Father Jean Baptiste Raverdy to oversee the expanding needs of Catholics in the area. The Reverend Machebeuf helped build St. Mary's Church in Denver, and with the help of Raverdy and other priests expanded the Catholic presence in Colorado all the way to Utah.

In 1868 Rome created Colorado and Utah as a separate vicariate, and Father Machebeuf was consecrated a bishop on August 16, 1868. In 1871 Utah was separated from the vicariate, and on August 18, 1887 the Holy See created the Diocese of Denver, which encompassed the entire state of Colorado.

Bishop Machebeuf died in 1889, but before he did he had succeeded admirably in laying a firm foundation of churches, missions, schools, social welfare and health-care organizations. He occasionally visited Colorado Springs and Colorado City. Among his contributions was the assignment of the first resident priests, Fathers W. J.

Finneran and Frederick Bender to Colorado Springs in 1877–a sign of its early growth and promise as a center of Catholic life. Each of Bishop Machebeuf's successors would build on this vision. Bishops Nicholas Matz (1889-1917), Joseph Tihen (1917-1931), Urban J. Vehr (1931-1967) and James V. Casey (1967-1986) would establish twenty-six of the current thirty-five parishes in the Colorado Springs diocese. A brief look at the early history of the parishes and institutions of the Denver era provides a sense of continuity between the early stream of Colorado Catholicism and what exists today in Colorado Springs.

■ *Bishop Joseph Projectus Machebeuf helped organize the Catholic presence in Colorado.*
© Archdiocese of Denver Archives, reprinted with permission

– Mining-era Catholicism –

Date	Parish	Location	County
1860	Manitou Mission	Colorado City	El Paso
1860	St. Joseph	Fairplay	Park
1875	St. Joseph	Salida	Chaffee
1877	St. Ann/St. Mary	Colorado Springs	El Paso
1879	Annunciation	Leadville	Lake
1880	St Rose of Lima	Buena Vista	Chaffee
1888	St. Francis	Castle Rock	Douglas
1889	O.L. Perpetual Help	Manitou	El Paso
1892	St. Peter	Cripple Creek	El Paso
1893	St. Mary/Sacred Heart	Colorado City	El Paso
1894	St. Victor	Victor	Teller
1899	St. Joseph	Leadville (Slovenian)	Lake
1901	St. Anthony of Padua	Hugo	Lincoln
1909	St. Augustine	Kit Carson	Chaffee
1910	St. Charles Borromeo	Stratton	Kit Carson
1911	St. Peter	Monument	El Paso
1915	St. Michael	Calhan	El Paso
1915	Ave Maria	Parker	Douglas
1916	St. Catherine	Burlington	Kit Carson
1917	Corpus Christi	Colorado Springs	El Paso
1918	Sacred Heart	Cheyenne Wells	Cheyenne
1920	St. Joseph	Fountain	El Paso
1925	St. Paul	Colorado Springs	El Paso
1925	Our Lady of Victory	Limon	Lincoln
1947	St. Mary	Flagler	Kit Carson
1948	Our Lady of Guadalupe	Colorado Springs	El Paso
1950	Divine Redeemer	Colorado Springs	El Paso
1955	Our Lady of the Woods	Woodland Park	Teller
1957	Holy Family	Security	El Paso
1959	Holy Trinity	Colorado Springs	El Paso
1965	Our Lady of the Pines	Black Forest	El Paso
1966	St. Joseph	Southgate	El Paso
1973	Holy Apostles	Colorado Springs	El Paso
1981	St. Andrew Kim	Colorado Springs	El Paso
1981	St. Patrick	Colorado Springs	El Paso

The Pikes Peak gold rush of 1858-1859 was the seminal event in the early history of Colorado. So also it played a role in the initial stages of Catholicism's institutional advance. Father Machebeuf offered his first Mass for miners in Colorado in Colorado City in 1860. Both he and Father Raverdy traveled to mining camps to celebrate the sacraments. Denver and Cherry Creek, Georgetown, Central City, Idaho Springs, Aspen and Fairplay are all communities that developed and expanded during this boom. Miners discovered substantial deposits of gold along the banks of California Gulch, and the area grew rapidly in the 1860s.

When the gold diggings played out abundant silver ore took its place as a source of wealth. In 1877 the few cabins on the banks of California Gulch were given the post office name of Leadville, and the little community thrived, boasting by 1880 a population of 15,000 and five churches. Irish miners formed one of these churches, Annunciation, which became an early hub of Catholic life. The magnificent church with elaborate altars and elegant stained glass was adorned with one of the highest steeples in the United States. Silver mining and later zinc continued the mining industry there. In 1883 Slovenian miners poured into the area and established their own national church named for St. Joseph. These two parishes held on as independent parishes until 1988 when they would be served by one pastor. In 2007, they were consolidated into one parish.

The discovery of gold by "Crazy Bob" Womack in the Cripple Creek area set off another important mineral rush in 1891. The riches eked from the ore of Cripple Creek created another generation of wealth and spawned a number of small towns. In 1892 Bishop Nicholas Matz sent Father Thomas Volpe to establish a church in Cripple Creek. On the highest hill in the city, he built St. Peter's Church and a school staffed by the Sisters of Mercy.

■ *Father Jean Baptiste Raverdy, friend and associate of Bishop Machebeuf, contributed substantially to the creation of a stable Catholic community in early Colorado.*
© Archdiocese of Denver Archives, reprinted with permission

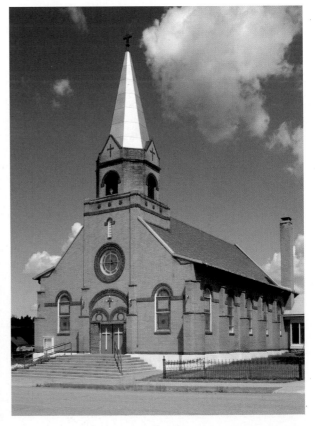

■ *Annunciation Church (red brick) and St. Joseph Church, Slovenian (cream brick) were two parish communities created for the miners of the area.*
© The Colorado Catholic Herald

17.

Another legacy of this mining rush was the little community of Victor. In 1894 Bishop Matz assigned Father Edward Downey as the first resident pastor to Victor. His twenty-one year pastorate of this community endeared him to all, including local Protestants, who sang his praises long after his death in 1918. Father Downey's priestly ministry in this bustling mining area reflected the kind of pragmatism common in the American West where Catholics were in the minority. Father Downey got along with everyone–poor and rich alike. He avoided ostentation in his personal life and in the life of the parish. He steadfastly refused to build a Catholic school, claiming that his own public school education taught him that children could receive a solid education in these institutions and not lose their faith. He learned the rhythms of life in the small mining community, and wisely did not install a chiming bell in St. Victor's tower for fear that its ring would wake one or the other of the men who worked in shifts in the mines and smelters. Cripple Creek and Victor felt the ebb and flow of the mining frontier as both parishes lost membership and support when mining played out in the 1920s. Eventually Our Lady of the Woods Parish in Woodland Park subsumed both parishes in 1955, and that is the status to this day.

The Cripple Creek district created a number of millionaires, among whom were Winfield Scott Stratton. Stratton poured a great deal of his considerable fortune into Colorado Springs. Of more direct benefit to the Catholic church was Spencer Penrose, whose ties to the church came when he married a widow, Julie Villiers Lewis McMillan, and settled in Colorado Springs.

Generous Benefactors: Spencer and Julie Penrose

Spencer Penrose, native of Philadelphia and a Harvard graduate, came west after earning his degree. He migrated to Colorado Springs from Las Cruces, New Mexico where he had run a fruit and produce company. He spent time in Cripple Creek "dabbling in many businesses," but it was mining that made him a huge fortune, selling his share in a mine, owning a mill trust and creating the Utah Copper Company. He eventually built the elaborate Broadmoor Hotel, which became one of the premier resort facilities in the area. Spencer loved Cheyenne Mountain (where he would one day be buried), and in 1901 met a young woman, Julie Villiers McMillan, at a party at the Cheyenne Mountain Country Club. McMillan's husband was dying of tuberculosis contracted during the Spanish American War. The daughter of a Detroit mayor, McMillan had two young children, Gladys and Jimmie. Her husband died in 1901, so also did her son Jimmie. She was widowed for five years when the nearly 40-year-old Penrose proposed to her. They married in April 1906 and enjoyed a happy life together. They had no children of their own, and built a romantic ranch house at Turkey Creek Ranch. In 1915, they bought a one-story Mediterranean home in an apple orchard constructed by Ashton Potters in 1910. The Penroses added two stories to the building, and Spencer named it "El Pomar de Mis Ojos" ("The Apple of My Eye") for his wife. It became their family residence and was known simply as El Pomar.

Julie Penrose had been baptized a Catholic but reared as an Episcopalian. Her daughter, Gladys married a Belgian nobleman Count Conet de Ways Ruart (Paul) and had one daughter, Pauline, on whom the Penroses doted. Paul was a devout Catholic and his infectious faith not only touched his wife, but his in-laws as well. Julie became interested in the church, and Spencer, whose religious heritage has been described as "completely unorthodox," followed. In 1919, in gratitude for the escape of the family from war-torn Belgium, Spencer Penrose built a "chapel of ease" in Broadmoor. Called the "Pauline Chapel," it is a modified replica of the Pauline Chapel of the Vatican and exquisitely adorned by statues and furnishings brought from Europe. Pauline married Baron Francois de Selys Longchamps and bore six children.

In 1931 Spencer Penrose began a nearly decade-long struggle with cancer and planned for the disposal of his estate. In December 1937 he created the El Pomar Foundation, which gave money to a wide array of projects that enhanced the quality of life in Colorado Springs. In 1941 the foundation made a donation to the Glockner Hospital and had it renamed Penrose Hospital. In 1944 the El Pomar estate was given to the Sisters of Charity who transformed it into a retreat house for women. Julie Penrose lived until 1956, quietly donating her husband's fortune to the up building of the region– and in particular to the Catholic church where she had found a spiritual home. Bishop Richard Hanifen suggests that her wealth may have played a role in keeping El Paso County within the boundaries of the Archdiocese of Denver when Colorado was divided into two dioceses in 1941. The Diocese of Pueblo, only thirty-five miles away from Colorado Springs, might have been the natural headquarters–but the sharp-minded Archbishop Vehr may have wanted to keep Julie Penrose as a benefactor within his domain.

Eastern Colorado:
Parishes in the Agricultural Heartland

Colorado Catholicism was heavily urban. However, the presence of the railroads virtually transformed all of Colorado. Cities such as Colorado Springs were tied to the lines for sustenance, so also were area farmers. Parochial life followed the rail lines.

The land itself was fertile and challenging. One anonymous clerical writer, explaining eastern Colorado to his bishop, wrote:

If you draw a straight line extending from a little south of Pueblo on to a little north of Denver and push that land east into Kansas and Nebraska you will cover what old geographies called the Great Colorado Desert. The Washington government examined this territory and found that in certain favorable seasons it could produce good crops, hence sometime in the early '90ties the territory was opened for settlement and certain attractive terms were offered to courageous spirits who aspired to the rank of the farming class. In addition, just about this time the steel business was losing its old time attraction–demand was falling and wages growing less. Hence we find a large number of the steel and rail workers forsaking this old avocation–coming to take up the government's offer–and ultimately settling around the little towns along the Rock Island.

Cattle ranching, various kinds of farming and agricultural pursuits were the mainstay of these communities. Pastors who worked here struggled to bring in the financial resources to keep alive the parishes, schools and mission stations.

The Union Pacific and Rock Island rail lines brought ministry to scattered Catholics between Denver and Colorado Springs and east to the Kansas line. Franciscans from St. Elizabeth's Parish in Denver took up the burden of ministry to the Catholics spread out across the Great Colorado Desert. Likewise, Benedictines from Pueblo also provided assistance. When the Franciscans could no longer sustain their ministry, they turned it over to Father Godfrey Raber and priests from Colorado Springs. Raber and a team of assisting priests ministered as best they could by taking long train rides to the stations and missions in the area including Burlington, Cheyenne Wells, Hugo and Limon.

The diocesan priests who took over from the Franciscans and the Pueblo Benedictines founded St. Michael in Calhan. A small Catholic community in Stratton formed in 1910. The Chicago-based Catholic Church Extension Society donated $1,000 for the first church in Stratton, St. Charles Borromeo, which did not have a resident pastor until the indomitable Reverend Alphonse C. Kieffer arrived in 1913. Father Kieffer, a native of Alsace-Lorraine, rode the rail lines to oversee missions in Hugo, Cheyenne Wells, Kit Carson, Wild Horse and Sheridan Lake and was able to raise funds for a school, staffed by the Sisters of Charity of the Blessed Virgin Mary until 1926. Later the Sisters of the Precious Blood assumed responsibility for the education of the parish youth. By 1901 the Franciscans had erected a small frame church in Hugo named for St. Anthony of Padua. In 1916 St. Catherine of Siena mission had been built in Burlington and remained a mission until 1949.

The Franciscans of Denver also ministered to the Catholic community of Kit Carson. In 1917-1918 St. Augustine Church was built. In 1919 Kieffer came to Kit Carson permanently and remained as pastor until 1950. In 1923 Father Michael Horgan took over St. Anthony in Hugo with its missions of Limon, Deertrail and Stasburg. Two years later, Our Lady of Victory was constructed in Limon with help from the Catholic Church Extension Society.

At Cheyenne Wells an elegant stone church was built along with a school staffed by the Sisters of the Holy Cross and later by the Sisters of St. Joseph of the Third Order of St. Francis. They continued this ministry until the school closed in 1971. A Catholic hospital for the area opened in 1947 and was run by the Sisters of St. Joseph. It served as a Catholic institution until December 1987 when it was transferred to Cheyenne County and renamed Cheyenne County Hospital.

Military Parishes

The placement of several military installations in the region fed El Paso County's wealth, growth and prominence. Colorado Springs's first military base, the Army's Camp Carson located near the south side of the city, opened in 1942. The army used the Colorado Springs Municipal Airport, later renamed Peterson Field, as a training base for bombers en route to World War II combat zones. A brief demobilization after the war led to a downturn in military investment in the area, but when hostilities erupted in Korea in 1950 Camp Carson sprang to life again.

In 1951 the United States Air Defense Command moved to Colorado Springs where it opened Ent Air Force Base. (Ent eventually closed down and was transformed into a United States Olympic Training Center.) Peterson Field, eventually renamed Peterson Air Force Base, would become the headquarters for the Air Force Space Command. In 1954 Camp Carson became Fort Carson, a permanent Army base. That same year the Eisenhower administration chose Colorado Springs as the site of the new Air Force Academy. In 1963 the North American Aerospace Defense Command (NORAD) was located in Cheyenne Mountain, and in 1983 Schriever Air Force Base (formerly Falcon Air Force Base) opened. These installations poured millions of dollars and brought hosts of new people into El Paso County.

Taken collectively, these military installations have contributed to the growth and cultural evolution of El Paso County. Uniformed military are everywhere. Important military functions–ranging from the active defense of the nation from missile attacks to Global Positioning Systems emanate from Colorado Springs. Thousands of tourists flock to the famous Air Force Academy chapel, designed by Chicago architect Walter A. Netsch, Jr.

Fort Carson, Peterson Air Force Base and of course the Air Force Academy all have chapels for Catholics and the services of full-time military chaplains. However, the presence of these important installations and the others in the area put pressure for expansion on existing parishes and helped create new ones. The comings and goings of military personnel has affected Catholic life. Frequently, retired military decide to make Colorado their home. Strong opinions on issues of war and peace have led to occasional friction between Catholics and local military personnel.

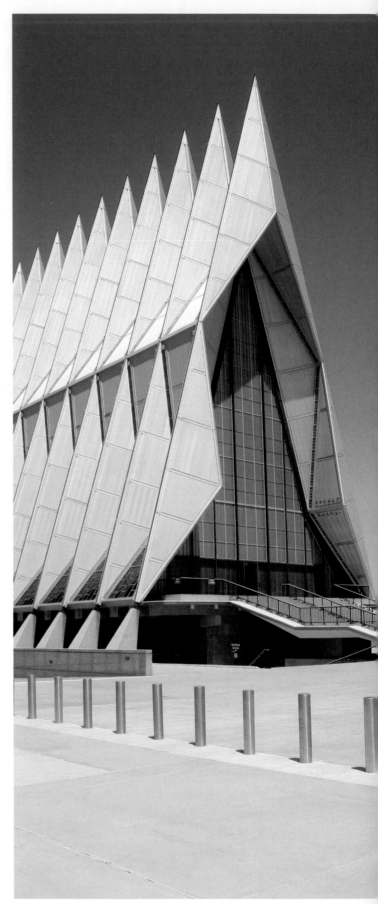

■ *USAFA Parish.*
© *John Glover*

Religious Communities of Women: Health Care and Schools

As they did in other parts of the country, religious women (sisters) sponsored and staffed important Catholic institutions. In 1885, three Sisters of Loretto, already working in Denver, arrived in Colorado Springs to open Loretto Academy, an elementary school for girls. Beginning in temporary quarters, by 1888 they had a new building and a growing number of students. This was originally an independent operation, separate from the city's St. Mary's Parish. Later, St. Mary, which had been located on several different sites, built a new church next to the growing academy.

■ *Bishop Nicholas Matz of Denver urged the Sisters of Charity to remain in Colorado Springs in order to provide health care.*
© Archdiocese of Denver Archives, reprinted with permission

Colorado Springs's reputation as a center for the cure of tuberculosis led to the foundation of Albert Glockner Memorial Tuberculosis Sanitarium in 1890. Founded by Marie Gwynne Glockner, the $26,000 Y-shaped facility was designed to optimize the full effects of sunshine then thought to have therapeutic value in curing the dreaded "white plague." Financial problems with the facility led Mrs. Glockner to appeal to the Sisters of Charity of Cincinnati to take over the facility in 1892. The Sisters too struggled with keeping the institution afloat, and in 1900 considered pulling out. However, Denver bishop Nicholas Matz prevailed on them to stay and its capable administrator, Sister Rose Alexius, insisted that the operation could work. In the end, the citizens of Colorado Springs helped eliminate the accumulated deficit on the facility. Financial security restored, the hospital began to expand, and eventually included a nursing school. In 1941 a gift from the El Pomar Foundation, underwrote a cancer research center. Renamed Penrose Hospital, the operation became the largest acute care hospital in Colorado Springs.

St. Francis Hospital began as a care facility for railroad workers of the Midland Railroad. The company purchased two adobe houses, and in 1877 the Franciscan Sisters of St. Francis Seraph of the Perpetual Adoration arrived from Lafayette, Indiana to staff the facility. The two buildings were soon inadequate, and the Sisters launched a campaign to build a larger facility known as St. Francis Hospital located on a hill between Colorado and Pikes Peak avenues. Expansion followed with the creation of a nursing school in 1919, and the upgrading and professionalization of service transformed St. Francis into a modern health-care facility. In 1987 the Penrose and St. Francis hospitals merged, and in 2005 ground was broken for a new hospital complex.

In 1952 the Franciscan Sisters received an old tuberculosis sanitarium as a bequest from the estate of Marguerite Davis. They transformed it into Mount St. Francis, a self-sufficient mother house for the newly-formed western province of their congregation. These Franciscans provided important leadership in areas of social justice, the environment and parish ministry for the diocese. The chapel of this mother house became the location of St. Francis Parish.

The Benedictine Sisters of Mount St. Scholastica in Atchison, Kansas began their ministry in Colorado in 1913 as teachers in elementary and secondary public schools of Antonito, Capulin and Conejos. They also staffed the Catholic school of St. Mary in Walsenbug. In 1960 the Atchison community purchased the seventeen-acre former San Luis Ranch for Girls on North Chelton Road in Colorado Springs. By 1963 the Sisters also ran Benet Academy and built a new school in 1966. Enrollments were healthy through the 1970s, but eventually declined. Financial burdens stemming back to the debt incurred to erect the building began to hit the community hard. In a six-day period of prayer and discernment, the Sisters decided to close Benet Academy at the end of the 1981-1982 academic year. The sisters had educated more than 680 girls.

In 1965 the Benedictine community had been raised to independent priory-monastery status, and in 1982 they were able to establish their Center at Benet Hill Monastery, where they offered a wide array of spiritual programs and pastoral services. In 1987 they built a new chapel complex, Our Lady of Peace Chapel. In 1966-1967, the convent purchased property in Black Forest, north of Colorado Springs, for a retreat center called Benet Pines. This facility offered retreats and a popular labyrinth. By 2001 there were only forty-five Benedictine Sisters, twenty-eight of them living and working at the Chelton Road complex. On July 24, 2001 the Sisters put the Chelton Hill property on the market. Prioress Rose Ann Barmann explained, "We really need a facility that fits a monastic charism. We're not a school; we're so much more than that. We're faith-filled women and we believe that this is a discerned decision that we've made."

Another small group of Benedictine nuns from Chicago came to staff St. Joseph's School in Salida in 1922. These indomitable Sisters withstood a considerable amount of anti-Catholic bigotry–even a cross burning on nearby Tenderfoot Mountain by an active chapter of the Ku Klux Klan. The growing school occupied most of their time, but their gradually declining numbers permanently ended their presence there in 1989.

Growth and the Future Diocese

Colorado's Catholic population grew slowly but steadily through the early 20th century. In 1941 the Holy See divided the state in two by creating a new diocese headquartered at Pueblo and encompassing the southern half of the state. This still left an enormous territory for the new Archdiocese of Denver, particularly in urbanizing areas around the major cities and near the key tourism areas of the state. Catholic growth around Colorado Springs was particularly fast-paced, thanks largely to the proliferation of military bases in the area. When Archbishop James V. Casey assumed the See of Denver in 1967, the pastoral care of those Catholics became an important priority.

■ *The Sisters of St. Francis of Perpetual Adoration have been an important part of the history of the Diocese of Colorado Springs.*
© *Sisters of St. Francis of Perpetual Adoration, St. Joseph Province, Mount St. Francis, Sister Michelle Micek*

■ Benedictine Sisters of Benet Hill, c. 1965
© Archives of the Benedictine Sisters, Benet Hill

Chapter 2

The Southern Vicariate:
A Diocese in Embryo

In a 1989 interview with the Colorado Springs *Gazette Telegraph*, Bishop Richard Hanifen spoke of his years at the Lateran University in Rome, where he studied canon law. Reporter Tom Morton wrote, "It was in Rome that Hanifen said he learned how Europeans unlike Americans value secrecy, and how that affects everything in Catholic life from confessions to the selection of bishops. 'The value of the individual,' commented Hanifen, 'is marked by the respect shown of keeping confidentiality.'" But if Bishop Hanifen saw the value of ecclesiastical discretion in his official church life, it was not evident that he, or those working with him, valued it as the best way to create a diocese. Although not initially clear that central Colorado would have a new diocese, once the decision was made the planning took place openly and with a great deal of consultation among a variety of people.

■ *Archbishop Urban J. Vehr of Denver presided over the tremendous growth of the Denver See especially after World War II.*
© *Archdiocese of Denver Archives, reprinted with permission*

Rethinking Colorado's Ecclesiastical Boundaries

Dealing with the rapid growth of northern Colorado fell to Archbishop James V. Casey, who succeeded Urban J. Vehr as Denver archbishop in 1967. Still in the midst of boom times, the Archdiocese of Denver needed new parishes and schools. In his quinquennial report of 1974, Archbishop Casey reported that he had created eighteen new parishes. "Colorado," he wrote Vatican officials, "has been identified as one of the three or four states within the United States that will experience the greatest growth within the next decade." He predicted that within the next five years he would have to create ten to fifteen parishes.

Even though the distance was relatively short and facilitated by the building of I-25, the travel between Denver and Colorado Springs had become increasingly time consuming. Colorado Springs, Bishop Hanifen later recalled, had already developed a sense of separation from the rest of the diocese. The local priests in the city bonded and met with each other regularly. For various reasons Colorado Springs had its own Catholic School Board and operated somewhat autonomously from the central Denver administration. Catholic Social Services (later Catholic Charities) had been incorporated in the city in 1970. One member of the Southern Vicariate who lived in Colorado Springs summed up the sense of distance between Denver and her local church: "Colorado Springs is united and separated from Denver. What works in Denver doesn't always work here even in business." Bishop Hanifen conceded that Colorado Springs felt like a step-child of Denver, and Archbishop Casey occasionally mentioned to him that people in Colorado Springs felt slighted and neglected by the Denver chancery.

As noted, Colorado Springs had not been attached to the newly-formed Diocese of Pueblo in 1941 probably because Archbishop Urban J. Vehr insisted on keeping El Paso County and the potential benefactions of the generous Julie Penrose within Denver's boundaries. Fast-growing El Paso County needed episcopal attention. Archbishop Casey already had one auxiliary, Bishop George Roche Evans, consecrated in 1969. In 1974, the same year of his quinquennial report and ad limina to Rome, Archbishop Casey petitioned the Vatican for a second auxiliary—his secretary, Father Richard C. Hanifen—to help him with his rapidly growing See.

■ *Archbishop James V. Casey began the initial planning for the future Diocese of Colorado Springs © Photo by the* Denver Catholic Register, *Archdiocese of Denver, reprinted with permission*

Richard Hanifen: Proto Bishop

Richard Charles Hanifen was born June 15, 1931, the third of four children of Edward A. Hanifen, Jr. and Dorothy Ranous, in Denver. A native son—he was steeped in the life and culture of the Centennial State. His Canadian grandfather, Edward Anselm Hanifen, Sr. had migrated to Leadville during the silver boom of the 1880s and owned properties that produced silver, lead and zinc. Hanifen's father was the cofounder of a leading Colorado investment firm. Young Hanifen attended St. Philomena's Parish and school in Denver. There he and his family met Monsignor William Higgins, who became a staunch family friend for years. In 1938, when one of Hanifen's siblings died at the age of 10 from leukemia, Monsignor Higgins helped the family through the painful crisis. Hanifen's mother recalled young Richard's love for radio comedy and that he and one of his brothers spent hours listening to Red Skelton and Bob Hope. She commented in an interview, "We were a busy but close family." Richard graduated from Regis High School in 1949. He majored in business at Regis University in 1953 and may have considered a professional career. A devout altar server in his early years, his decision to become a priest after college did not take his family completely by surprise. He entered St. Thomas Seminary in Denver in 1953 and was ordained by Archbishop Vehr in June 1959. He also finished a master's degree in theology at the Catholic University in Washington, D.C., that same summer. Father Hanifen spent a summer as an assistant at Our Lady of the Mountains Parish in Estes Park, and then in the fall joined the full-time staff of the Cathedral of the Immaculate Conception. He also taught religion in the Cathedral high school. Archbishop Vehr sent Father Hanifen and five other priests to the Catholic University for training as school counselors. To comply with state requirements, which required a degree or its equivalency, Vehr permitted the priests to study during the summer months. It took six summers to finish the master's degree in counseling. Archbishop Vehr next sent Father Hanifen to the Lateran University in Rome to study for a licentiate in canon law. Hanifen offered to stay in Rome for a doctorate, but the new archbishop, James V. Casey, called him home. Father Hanifen's background in canon law became a valuable asset when he was called on to found the Colorado Springs diocese. His mastery of the code and his awareness of the options it gave a diocesan bishop in meeting the spiritual needs of the people would be put to work many times over. His knowledge of the law was always good–but he eschewed the sometimes stuffy and legalistic persona that

often attached to chancery canonists. For Hanifen law was a means to an end. His working motto appeared to be the old saw, *suprema lex, salus animarum* (the highest law, the salvation of souls).

Father Hanifen reported to his new superior who invited him to work in the chancery. Asked if Father Hanifen had any preconditions to the work, the young priest requested to live in a parish and to have Wednesdays off. Archbishop Casey and Father Hanifen "clicked," and Hanifen served Casey loyally as secretary and chancellor of the archdiocese–even occasionally golfing with his "boss." He held the post until selected as an auxiliary bishop in 1974.

Father Hanifen's earliest years of priesthood were caught up with the preparations for and the experience of Vatican II. His two years in Rome took place during the aftermath of the Council, and it was evident that the Council's spirit and letter helped shape his understanding of church life, theology and his views of authority. When he returned home in 1968, he found a country and church in the midst of social upheaval. Hanifen did not claim to be prophetic or out of the ordinary, but later noted that in the early 1960s he didn't trouble himself "with questions about Vatican II and the future of the church, the civil rights movement or the Vietnam War." He continued, "I was never out front on anything. I was a little embarrassed that priests and nuns were marching." The mood of the country was suspicious of authority–secular and ecclesiastical. Exposés of the hypocrisy and deviousness of national political leaders fueled the demands for transparency and greater accountability from leaders in every walk of life. In Catholic circles, the issuance of the papal encyclical *Humanae Vitae* (1968) banning any form of artificial contraception had set off a firestorm of opposition from theologians and clergy "in the trenches." Many lay persons not only objected to the ban but also to the pope's rejection of advice from the majority of a hand-picked commission, which urged a rethinking of church teaching on the subject. Demands for "collegiality," consultation and shared governance of church affairs flourished at this time. Even moderately liberal bishops like Casey occasionally found themselves accused of insensitivity and of dragging their feet on needed reforms.

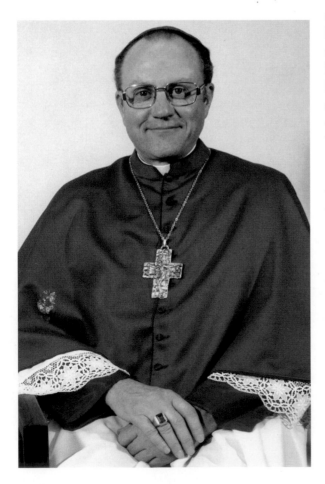

■ *Auxiliary Bishop Richard C. Hanifen*
© *Photo by James Baca,* Denver Catholic Register,
Archdiocese of Denver, reprinted with permission

As Archbishop Casey's private secretary, Father Hanifen knew well the travails and struggles of the prelate and of the archdiocese. He no doubt ushered many a priest into the archbishop's office who came to announce his resignation or impending marriage. Hanifen wrote sermons and speeches for Casey, and also helped to shield him from various militants, including a Theatine priest who set the lobby of the chancery on fire as an act of protest. Father Hanifen genuinely admired Casey's patience and resolve, even though he did not share the shy and taciturn personality of his superior. Hanifen closely observed both Casey's and auxiliary bishop George Evans's efforts to engage the social issues and challenges of the day. He imitated Archbishop Casey's efforts to be consultative and collaborative—two emphases that he felt flowed from the conciliar emphasis on collegiality. Hanifen was a pleasant and extroverted man, who spoke intelligently without notes and conveyed a sense of warmth that seemed novel for bishops in those days. Hanifen skied the slopes of Colorado and strummed a guitar now and then and was generally liked by his peers.

Hanifen was appointed titular bishop of Abercorn and consecrated an auxiliary bishop of Denver on September 20, 1974. Bishop Hanifen's enthusiastic embrace of Vatican II's emphasis on collegiality was coupled by his love and respect for the growing Spanish-speaking culture in Denver. A former cursillista his episcopal motto was taken from the opening lines of the popular Cursillo anthem, "De Colores." He explained that the phrase was "rich in meaning for me and many others...it is a phrase of joy. It is intended to express the simple, but some-

times elusive truth that our lives become 'colorful' and joyful when we are free and willing to become receivers of God's beauty and love in all facets of our lives."

Bishop Hanifen did not really have time to settle into the pattern of confirmations, cornerstone blessings and banquets handed off to auxiliaries. On January 7, 1976 Casey appointed Hanifen Vicar of the southern region–basically the urbanizing area around Colorado Springs. With this came his assignment to the pastorate of St. Mary's Church. Hanifen related the decision to create the Southern Vicariate in a retrospective interview given after the death of Archbishop Casey in March 1986. "I was with him [Casey] at the time we were down here–it must have been 1970–when Monsignor Robert Hoffman drove Archbishop Casey and myself out toward what is now Village Seven and showed us a model home on a dirt tract. There wasn't another building anywhere. We looked at that and we talked about a new satellite church for Divine Redeemer. Archbishop Casey said this ought to become a vicariate." It took nearly six years for this vision to become a reality. "I wasn't too crazy about Colorado Springs because they always seemed to criticize what we were doing in Denver; they felt all we wanted was their money," he confided to a reporter. However, after a few months of listening to the locals, he concluded that they had some valid points, "We [the church leadership in Denver] ...were not paying attention." In addition to his parochial duties, Hanifen provided an episcopal presence in a part of the Denver Archdiocese that did not often see a mitered head process down its church aisles. People and priests welcomed him warmly–but with reservations at first.

■ *Bishop Hanifen sought the good will and support of influential local clerics like Father Omer Foxhoven of Divine Redeemer Church.*
© Photo by Denver Catholic Register, Archdiocese of Denver, reprinted with permission

A New Diocese: To Be or Not To Be

Bishop Hanifen had been unaware of the plans for creating the Diocese of Colorado Springs. As a priest-secretary, he had never attended province meetings where these things were discussed, and the close-mouthed Archbishop Casey had not divulged anything in their occasionally long car rides. Hence, Hanifen divided his early time, devoting attention to the pastoral care of the thriving St. Mary's Church, the oldest and largest in Colorado Springs, and to local situations that required closer episcopal attention than Denver could give.

Hanifen worked hard to gain the trust of the priests in Colorado Springs and adopted the stance of a benevolent co-worker. He recalled that two priests in the city possessed genuine spiritual leadership abilities. One was Father Omer Foxhoven at Divine Redeemer, described as a very spiritual and creative pastoral leader. The other was the bluntly honest Theatine Father Francis Colom, pastor of Our Lady of Guadalupe Church. Foxhoven and Colom were initially suspicious of bishops, but both invited Hanifen to visit regularly. Other clergy in the area proved to be supportive as well, including Father Theodore Haas with whom Hanifen had resided in Denver when he served on the chancery staff and Father Edward Madden, pastor of Holy Trinity Parish. Bishop Hanifen had contacts among the religious congregations of women. He received a very warm welcome from laity, who were, in his recollection, "delighted to have a bishop around." In 1981, he managed to recruit Father John Slattery an old priest friend from Denver who founded the new parish of St. Patrick in Colorado Springs. As a sign that the two areas were slowly drifting apart, the mini-drama over Slattery's appointment unfolded. Bishop Hanifen recalled that rather than ask Casey directly, he put Slattery's name before the Denver Personnel Board and lobbied for the priest's reassignment. Casey allowed Slattery's transfer, but was irked by what looked like "priest pilfering" from one diocese to another.

Whatever Bishop Hanifen did in those early years worked. Archbishop Casey reported to the Holy See in 1978 about the Hanifen appointment and the vicariate.

In this capacity Bishop Hanifen has undertaken an administrative and financial reorganization of the Catholic school system in Colorado Springs and coordinated efforts to provide adequate resources for expansion of parish facilities. Under his direction the lines of communication between central archdiocesan administration in Denver and parish communities of the southern area have been strengthened and improved.

Over time, it became evident that the Southern Vicariate was the staging ground for the future Diocese of Colorado Springs. Until Rome formally erected the new See on November 10, 1983, Bishop Hanifen kept a foot in both worlds—the rapidly growing and increasingly autonomous counties of the vicariate and also in the Denver See.

The Wider Context: U.S. and Catholic Life in the 1970s

The 1970s are still so close to us that it is really impossible to have any true historical perspective on the era. However, some tentative observations on the key events of the era help us better contextualize the origins of the Colorado Springs diocese.

The long Vietnam War came to a formal end in January 1973 when the United States and North Vietnamese reached a fragile accord, allowing the United States to withdraw the remainder of its troops. The war had become an increasingly divisive issue in American political and public life. President Richard Nixon and his chief foreign policy advisor, Henry Kissinger, sought to achieve "peace with honor." Dramatic diplomatic openings to Communist China and the Soviet Union were part of larger efforts to bring an end to the conflict. With the phase out of American troops, the collapse of American-supported regimes in Cambodia and South Vietnam followed. In 1975 Vietnam fell to the Communist regime of the north.

The lingering effects of the war and all that had kept it going contributed to the cultural mix of the era. Trust in government leaders was one casualty of the war. Further damage was done by the Watergate scandal—a number of illegal activities emanating from the Nixon White House. The resignations of Vice President Spiro T. Agnew in 1973 and in 1974 President Richard Nixon—and the latter's subsequent pardon by President Gerald Ford—enhanced a mood of distrust about the government and authority in general. In 1976 the election of the smiling governor of Georgia, Jimmy Carter, raised hopes for something better. Carter's victory also symbolized a rekindling of evangelical fervor as the new president advertised his "born-again" beliefs. American life and culture continued to celebrate the individualism of people, including an increase in consumption—but also awakened people to limits on natural resources like oil and other forms of energy. Economic downturns and increasing monetary inflation—much of it fueled by higher energy costs—kept people on edge and finances precarious.

Concurrently, American Catholics consolidated the changes made by Vatican II. Liturgical reform continued apace with modifications in the missal and the sacramentary—and the increase of lay participation as Extraordinary Ministers of Holy Communion. Adult catechetical programs flourished with eager Catholics taking courses in scripture, liturgy and even church history. The revivification of the Rite of Christian Initiation of Adults (RCIA) gave promise of a new approach to adult Catholic life. A newly retooled and empowered National Conference of Catholic Bishops developed major statements and policies on issues confronting not only internal church affairs, but also national and international issues.

Belgian Archbishop Jean Jadot, Apostolic Delegate to the United States from May 1973 to June 1980, influenced the selection of bishops in this era. Working with the bishop's conference, he selected men more "pastoral" in their approach to episcopal ministry. These Jadot-era prelates, for the most part, favored lay cooperation, took the time and energy to be collaborative with their priests and flocks, and avoided, where possible, coercive approaches to most issues. Many bishops of this era symbolically shed the imperial trappings of their office—selling off fancy mansions and moving into cathedral rectories. Many expanded diocesan services to meet new needs in catechesis, family life ministries, social justice and public relations. A visit to a diocesan headquarters was no longer "a trip to the chancery" or to the marriage tribunal, but rather to a "pastoral center."

Major changes in priestly formation stressed the practicum experiences for seminarians. One of the key innovations was Clinical Pastoral Education (CPE), which became a requirement in many American seminaries. Seminarians were sent to work in hospitals and health-care facilities where they gained not only practical experience with the gritty issues of life and death but also the critical introspection of what they did and why they did it. Many seminaries also inserted a year of pastoral internship so seminarians could become acquainted with the diversity and demands of a typical Catholic congregation. Changes in seminary curricula stressed historical approaches to systematic theology and liturgy and wrestled with evolving ideas on moral and medical issues. Scripture study became extremely popular as future priests explored the richness of the bible with trained scholars who walked them through the challenges and excitement of various interpretations. It was hoped that seminarians would enter the ministry not only with a firm grounding in the basics of Catholic belief, but also with a deep sense of service to the People of God. Seminarians were urged to avoid excessive preoccupation with clerical identity and "power" and to be prepared for the unexpected challenges of a typical parish or special ministry. Many new priests came out of their studies with the same suspicion of authority as their secular contemporaries. Occasionally clashing "theologies" and understandings of liturgy, clerical life and common living created tensions between older and younger priests.

The other reality of clerical life during this period was the decline of priestly vocations. Although the large-scale resignations of priests seemed to have peaked in the early 1970s, the steady dropping away of the ordained continued every year. Seminary classes continued to decline and even though lay persons were admitted to seminaries to study for theological degrees, a number of them, including Denver's own St. Thomas Seminary, had to close their doors.

Another major thrust of the 1970s was the growing visibility and presence of women in positions of leadership in the American church. During the 1960s, American society experienced a new wave of feminism that reshaped understandings of gender roles and put pressure on social institutions to end perceived discrimination against women. The winds of this movement were also felt within churches, which began to select women as leaders and install them in positions of authority. In 1976 the Episcopal Church in the United States broke ground when they ordained a number of women to the priesthood. When a similar demand surfaced in the Roman Catholic church, Popes Paul VI and John Paul II explicitly ruled out the ordination of women to the priesthood. Nonetheless, many bishops and clergy wanted to include women in more and more of the leadership positions in the church and to make sure that their insights and wisdom were part of collective decisions. Religious women (sisters) often took the lead. Many of them, well-trained academically and pastorally, stepped forward to create a space for themselves within the male leadership of the Catholic Church. Many Sisters, earlier trained as educators or nurses, found their skills put to use in parish and diocesan religious education programs, school superintendencies and different levels of diocesan leadership. As time went on, Catholic women sought increasingly more visible roles in church life and leadership–including pastoral duties in parishes.

Lay empowerment had been increasing apace as well. From expanded roles in liturgical ministry to taking the lead in religious education, laymen and laywomen embraced the spirit of collegiality modeled by the Vatican Council. Church structures were called on to be more collaborative. Parish councils popped up in many places; diocesan pastoral councils offered advice to bishops. The high point of lay activism came with the convocation of the 1976 Detroit Call to Action Conference, which brought thousands together to forge strong church positions on a variety of issues.

Finally, religious movements–many of them lay-based–emerged and dominated the scene for a time. Cursillos, a short course in Christianity enjoyed great popularity with clergy and laity. Marriage Encounter–a program to revivify marriages began its slow, steady ascent as a popular program for Catholic couples. Even more visible was the Charismatic Renewal–a Catholic version of the Pentecostal movements in Evangelical Protestantism–replete with gifts of tongues, healing and hands-uplifted prayer. Catholic charismatic renewal was "born" at Duquesne University in Pittsburgh in 1969. It soon developed "centers" of visible activity at the University of Notre Dame, Ann Arbor (Michigan) and San Francisco. Charismatic prayer groups led by priests, women religious and lay persons popped up all across the country. Popular spiritual authors like Jesuit John Powell, Henri Nouwen and Richard Rohr, OFM, wrote best-selling books and lectured widely around the country. Religious seekers trekked to contemplative monasteries and convents for silent retreats and spiritual introspection.

The Catholic mood of the 1970s, and even the early 1980s, was still caught up in the enthusiasm generated by Vatican II. Many Catholic leaders valued collaboration and consultation as a way of governance, and many were eager to hear fresh ideas and interpretations of scripture, receptive to the revised liturgy and especially to new music and liturgical expressions. Lay ministry became more and more accepted as a logical outpouring of a renewed understanding of baptism and confirmation. Not everything was smooth and orderly, and a certain level of tension existed as various parishes and dioceses tried to work out the challenges. Some met with success, while others sometimes became mired in unpleasant public controversies and polarization. These general trends provided the context for the formative years of the Colorado Springs diocese.

Slouching Toward a New Diocese

Eventually it became clear that Colorado Springs would be the hub of a new diocese. Once aware, Bishop Hanifen began to plan for this eventuality. By nature he was inclined to consult a great deal before making decisions and sought to include as many people as he could. Early upon taking over as Vicar, he had assembled a Vicariate Pastoral Council and team to assess the needs of the area and to discuss issues of concern. The Pastoral Council was composed of six lay people, three priests and three sisters who began meeting on a regular basis. The council was useful for bouncing ideas around and dreaming dreams, but planning for a new diocese required full-time people who could create an administrative infrastructure. The early bureaucracy of the vicariate had been simple–in part because of financial constraints and the existence of similar offices in Denver, still technically in control. Bishop Hanifen favored a "team" approach. His clearest priority was the pastoral service of the people–in particular, to free up clergy so they could tend to the needs of their communities. He himself was not an administrative kind of bishop–preferring instead to be out meeting people, praying with them (he accepted countless invitations from a host of different groups) and relied on his staff to carry on the day-to-day business of the vicariate.

The team included his closest advisors. Among them was Servite Sister Jeanine Percy who headed up the Vicariate for Ministry Services. Percy hailed from the Chicago area and had joined the Servite Sisters in Ladysmith, Wisconsin in 1959. She was an educator from the start, teaching math and science to high school students and securing an advanced degree in Religious Studies. In 1969 she began her career as an educational administrator in the Diocese of Superior, Wisconsin. In 1977 she moved to Colorado Springs, where she was invited to direct the Southern Area Religious Education Center of the Archdiocese of Denver. Sister Percy would oversee religious education aspects of the vicariate. Sister Maryanna Coyle, a Sister of Charity, oversaw Catholic schools until she departed in 1981.

In late 1979 Bishop Hanifen hired Benedictine Sister Patricia McGreevy as coordinator of Planning and Canonical Services. McGreevy came, admirably qualified with a master's degree in Church Administration, a Licentiate in canon law, years of experience as an educator, and having held positions of responsibility in her religious community, the Benedictine Sisters of Erie, Pennsylvania. A classmate had urged her to apply for the position, and Bishop Hanifen found her skills exactly

■ *Benedictine Sister Patricia McGreevy, a trained canonist with strong skills in planning, played an important role in the creation of the Diocese of Colorado Springs.*
© Benedictine Sisters of Erie, PA

what he needed. McGreevy set up a local marriage tribunal to facilitate the processing of annulments emanating in the Colorado Springs area. In addition to her canon law expertise, Sister McGreevy had experience in needs assessment, program development and long-range planning–all skills the bishop would need and use in the formation of the new diocese. Rounding out the team was Tom Cotterill, the director of Catholic Community and Youth Services.

Bishop Hanifen and his team completed the remote preparations for the vicariate's future diocesan status. Adapting strategic planning and goal-setting techniques in wide use among religious congregations, dioceses and parishes across the United States, the group devised questionnaires to plumb the needs and aspirations of the vicariate's various constituencies. What was the make-up of the church in this area? What were the priorities of the Catholic church in this part of Colorado? Where did they want the church to go? Every step of this process seemed to be out in the open, and understood by most of the participants. Keeping everyone informed became not only the task of Bishop Hanifen, but also of a special "Pikes Peak Edition" of the *Denver Catholic Register*. Headed by John and Joanne Pearring, this important and well-designed Catholic newspaper reported faithfully on the progress of the Southern Vicariate, running regular stories on the region's parishes and creating a sense of solidarity among these communities.

Bishop Hanifen's extroverted charm and unpretentious style helped weld the vicariate together and prepared it for organizational transition to diocesan status. Hanifen seemed to be everywhere: sacramental celebrations in parishes; socials and other events in the Catholic community; also in civic organizations. Lea Roads, a member of the Vicariate Pastoral Council spoke of the peripatetic bishop, "I often meet him at the Chamber and other functions. He has high visibility which is essential for leadership."

Like the other Denver auxiliary, Bishop George R. Evans, Bishop Hanifen spoke out on social issues–even at the risk of ruffling feathers among the laity. For example in April 1982, he openly criticized the persecution of missionaries in El Salvador, the nuclear arms race and capital punishment–all issues likely to be somewhat neuralgic for the very conservative populace of Colorado Springs many of whom were staunch Republicans and supporters of President Ronald Reagan. But unlike the sometimes blunt Evans, Hanifen's words were always more measured and balanced. He had a way of speaking that made a point, but also left people with the sense that others of good will might take another approach. Bishop Hanifen also struck up friendships with local rabbis and ministers. True to the spirit of Vatican II, he wisely chose to accentuate the things religious groups agreed upon rather than their divisions–a diplomatic gesture in a community that was on the way to becoming an Evangelical Vatican.

■ *Bishop George Roche Evans, auxiliary of Denver is pictured here presiding at Mass. Evans was a strong voice for social justice in the archdiocese.*
© *Photo by the* Denver Catholic Register, *Archdiocese of Denver, reprinted with permission*

A Crossroads Moment

With all this obvious organizational activity many expected that the announcement of a new See was right around the corner. In fact, it took longer than expected–which created some consternation among clergy and others. What took so long?

Some of the delay related to the failure of an original plan. The decision to create the Colorado Springs diocese was only part of a grander scheme devised by Archbishop Casey to reconfigure the ecclesiastical jurisdictions of the entire state. Since 1941 there had only been two dioceses in the state, Denver and Pueblo. The division had worked well for a time, but the rapid growth and demographic shifts in Colorado created conditions for a rethinking of existing boundaries. Casey, like others of the time, believed that smaller dioceses were more pastorally effective than larger ones where auxiliary bishops did much of the day-to-day sacramental work. He was likewise sensitive to the frequent laments that sections–mostly rural or remote areas–of large dioceses felt neglected and ignored by the central administration. In late 1979 after Pueblo bishop Charles Buswell announced his retirement, Archbishop Casey felt that an opportune moment to review the diocesan boundaries had come. He subsequently announced at a meeting of 100 church leaders, "I want to begin the discussion on Colorado Springs becoming a separate diocese in the state of Colorado."

Bishop Buswell's successor in Pueblo, Bishop Arthur Tafoya, agreed with Archbishop Casey's plan, and the prelates sketched out a major reconfiguration of diocesan boundaries, creating a new diocese for the Fort Collins-Greeley area and the Western Slope-Grand Junction area. Colorado Springs was to be part of this reorganization. The hope was that residential bishops could be more accessible to their constituents and priests. Reorganization would also make the Archdiocese of Denver much more manageable. However, this ambitious redesign of Catholic Colorado hit insurmountable difficulties related to the local economy. The Grand Junction diocese fell by the wayside when Exxon Mobil, an economic mainstay of the region, abruptly pulled out of the oil shale business leaving economic devastation in its wake. This made it impossible for the assembled counties to produce enough revenue to sustain even a modest diocesan organization. Fort Collins never even made it to the planning stage–no doubt due to local economic conditions. This left only Colorado Springs, allegedly slated to be the second of the newly created Sees, as the remnant of this once grand plan. Here too, the health of the local economy became an issue. When the equivalent of a feasibility study for the diocese was submitted to a committee of American bishops some worried that the particular configuration of counties would not have enough financial or human resources to support diocesan structure.

However, while Bishop Hanifen and others took note of the financial and personnel issues, they also stressed the greater priority of the pastoral needs of the area–needs not being met by the Denver See. Others in the area, priests and lay persons, continued to grumble about their "step-child" status. Bishop Hanifen met this also among the farmers and ranchers along the Great Plains who rarely saw a bishop and groused that all Denver wanted was their money.

The delays caused by this internal debate created some morale problems among the clergy. The logjam was finally broken by the Apostolic Pro-Nuncio, Pio Laghi, who insisted that Pope John Paul II liked small dioceses. On November 10, 1983 the Holy See announced the creation of the Diocese of Colorado Springs–with 26

■ *Archbishop Casey, pictured here in his later years, devised a grand scheme to reorganized the diocesan boundaries of the entire state of Colorado. The Diocese of Colorado Springs was a part of his larger plans.*
© Photo by the Denver Catholic Register, *Archdiocese of Denver, 17.139.75-reprinted with permission*

parishes and ten counties, nine clipped off from Denver and one from Pueblo. Bishop Hanifen explained, "We are quite small compared to the traditional diocese. But this is the result of a trend stated by Pope John Paul." Father Owen McHugh, pastor of Divine Redeemer Parish, expressed gratitude and a sense of relief. "We've been waiting a long time. A lot of structure is worked through already. This whole process has been going on for awhile."

Creating the Boundaries

The nucleus of the new diocese were the counties under the Southern Vicariate. But added to them were the mountain towns of Leadville, Buena Vista and Salida, which lie in a row along the Arkansas River. These included the parishes of St. Joseph and Annunciation in Leadville, St. Joseph in Salida and St. Rose of Lima in Buena Vista with its mission–St. Joseph in Fairplay. Buena Vista and Salida had been in the Pueblo diocese. The choice of the ten counties had been based on geographical location. Douglas County was problematic. As part of Denver's metropolitan area, Douglas County Catholics already attended Denver area parishes and schools. A plan was discussed to give half to Denver and half to Colorado Springs. However, Rome balked at violating county lines, and Archbishop Casey agreed

to give it to Colorado Springs. In effect, the new diocese is drawn according to a straight line from the Continental Divide to the Kansas border. This encompasses the counties of Chafee, Cheyenne, Douglas, Elbert, El Paso, Kit Carson, Lake, Lincoln, Park and Teller, consisting of 15,560 square miles in all. Sister McGreevy summed up the challenge best noting:

> The diversity of populations encompassed by these boundaries was indeed a challenge: ranchers in the plains; miners, ranchers, ski industry in the west; metropolitan profile in the urban areas of Colorado Springs; the bedroom community of Denver in the north. The distances that had to be covered to travel to these three sections of the diocese were problematic and worsened with the rising median age and diminishing clergy population factored in. The need to unify, to build a common vision of the church, to attend to diverse pastoral needs of such different populations impacted the motivating goals that [Hanifen] had for the new diocese and the clergy who served it.

Although the new diocese faced some serious obstacles, the pastoral care of these diverse communities would receive attention. The new diocese had been launched.

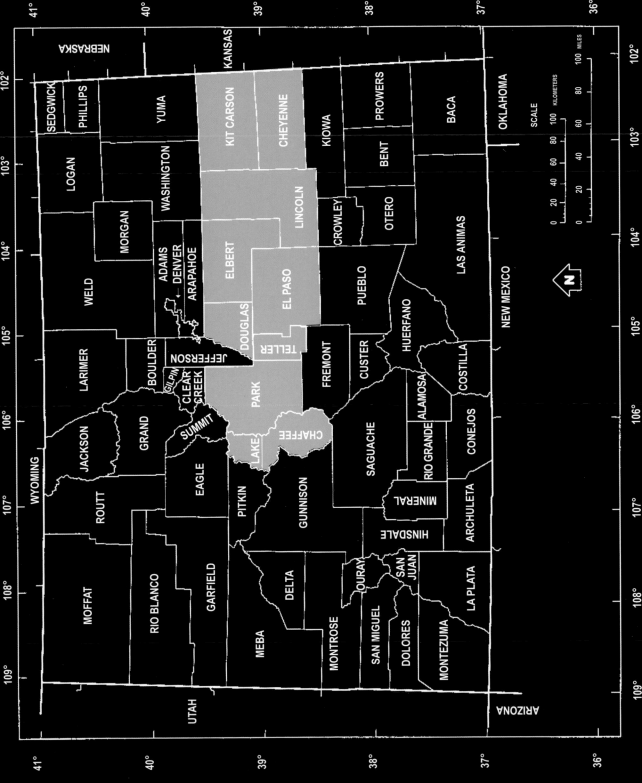

Chapter 3

Come Let Us Climb the Mountain of the Lord:
The First Ten Years (1984-1994)

"We're trying to keep it as simple as possible," said Sister Pat McGreevy, speaking of Bishop Hanifen's plans for the installation liturgy on January 30, 1984. But as she contemplated the presence of more than thirty bishops, all processing into the Pikes Peak Center to witness the formal seating of Bishop Hanifen on the portable cathedra, she acknowledged that "much of Bishop Hanifen's desire for simplicity will be beneath the surface." Benedictine Sister Anne Stedman coordinated the hour and a half liturgy, which welcomed Apostolic Pro-Nuncio Pio Laghi, and included readings from Isaiah, Romans and the 17th chapter of St. John. A moment of tension occurred when the time came for the reading of the papal bull formally creating the new diocese. At the critical moment, the bull could not be found. To lighten the moment Hanifen quipped, "This is cattle country and we have never lost a bull yet." The missing document was produced and following the ceremony, a four-hour reception took place at the Antlers Hotel where Bishop Hanifen pumped the hands of many well-wishers.

"Ad Montem Sanctam Tuum," Hanifen had emblazoned on the new diocesan crest—"To Your Holy Mountain." The next eighteen years would be filled with both the mountain tops and the valley bottoms of Catholic life.

Bishop Hanifen needed no tutorials on the realities of the new See. He knew the clergy and history of many of the parishes. Leadville, for example, where his own family had made their fortune was a divided community with two separate ethnic churches and a dwindling Catholic population. Salida and Buena Vista in Chaffee County, inherited from the Diocese of Pueblo, and its clergy felt a bit like ducks out of water. Farmers and ranchers on the eastern Plains always lived on the cusp of financial ruin and yet cherished the land, their work and the closeness of their communities. They had high hopes that they would see more of the bishop. Older areas like Cripple Creek and Victor whose mining deposits had played out, soon found a new form of wealth in gambling casinos. All of the areas of the new diocese may have lamented Denver's "neglect," but the absence of diocesan control and officials had also created a sense of autonomy that many enjoyed.

Bishop Hanifen made good on promises to be more visible in the remote areas of the diocese, but the challenges presented to him came mostly from the rapid growth in the urbanizing area of Colorado Springs–fueled by industry (firms like Lockheed, Ford, IBM and MCI) and the military. The area was politically and socially conservative–factors reinforced by the growing presence of evangelical churches. In fact, the Catholic Church was probably the most liberal institution in the community. The challenge of Douglas County–the fastest growing county in the United States for seven years running–only kept expanding. As noted, Douglas County Catholics were already members of Denver area parishes. Providing for their spiritual needs with new churches and schools, and cementing their loyalty to the new diocese required a great deal of time and effort–all of which took place against the backdrop of important changes in the American Catholic community.

■ *Archbishop Pio Laghi,*
Apostolic Delegate and Pro-Nuncio to
the United States (1980-1984) played
an important role in the creation of the
Diocese of Colorado Springs
© Catholic News Service

Catholic Life in the 1980s

Much was beginning to change in the 1980s. On the secular front, the presidencies of Jimmy Carter and Ronald Reagan signaled the revival of a long moribund conservative movement–fueled by a backlash against the excesses of the 1960s and 1970s, a rehabilitation of laissez-faire economics, and a desire to restore America's slipping status in the aftermath of the Vietnam War and the Iranian hostage crisis. Reagan, who was re-elected in a 1984 landslide, appealed to some religiously motivated voters, including Catholics, with a strategic conversion to anti-abortion politics even though he had signed one of the nation's first abortion liberalization laws when he was governor of California in the 1960s. Under his administration, the United States began a major arms buildup and took a militant stance against perceived communist insurgencies in Central America and Afghanistan. Americans seemed to love the ever genial and sunny actor even when they discovered his administration was selling arms to Iranian militants and using the proceeds to fund Nicaraguan counter-revolutionaries. Although the final collapse of the Soviet Empire did not take place on Reagan's watch, when the "evil empire" did fall, many cited Reagan's toughness with the Soviets as a major cause.

In the Catholic Church, a period of transition arrived during the tumultuous year of the three popes–1978. The death of Paul VI and the election of his short-lived successor, John Paul I, ushered in a new era. On October 16, 1978 the Cardinal Archbishop of Krakow, Karol Cardinal Wojtyla was elected to the See of Peter. The novelty of this non-Italian and youngish pontiff (58-years-old at the time) initially impressed the world. But no one was prepared for the directions in which this charismatic and forceful pontiff would take the church during his twenty-six year reign. He began his ministry with a vigor and verve not seen in the papacy in modern times. Pope John Paul II endeared himself to the world through a regimen of more than 100 international trips and spectacular public masses and ceremonies held on every continent of the world. His support of the struggling Solidarity movement in his native Poland contributed to the final collapse of the Soviet domination of Eastern Europe. He forged ecumenical ties with the East, prayed with people of all faith traditions in two memorable sessions at Assisi, preached in Rome's synagogue and toward the end of his life visited Jerusalem's Wailing Wall. His courage in surviving a 1981 assassination attempt and his public forgiveness of the man who shot him brought tears to the eyes of millions. John Paul II inspired a generation of Catholics young and old by his

warmth, charisma and personal charm. Pope John Paul traveled to America on several occasions, including one to World Youth Day held at Cherry Creek State Park in Colorado. At his 2005 funeral millions thronged Rome to say farewell and chanted "Santo Subito"–a saint now– restoring an old tradition of the acclamation of saints by the people themselves.

Pope John Paul II had some misgivings about the direction of events in the aftermath of Vatican II and intended to correct them. He delegated details and the implementation of this policy to trusted administrators. His key appointment to the Congregation of the Doctrine of the Faith, Cardinal Joseph Ratzinger, moved quickly to reimpose discipline and uniformity on Catholic life and teachings, which many believed had gone astray. This included disciplining dissident theologians and insisting that priests stay out of secular politics. Ratzinger and others shifted the notion of collegiality away from a democratic concept where everyone should have a say–to a more hierarchical model where laity and lower-level clergy should cooperate in their proper sphere under the leadership of the bishops and in firm union with the Holy See. An important part of this program of "restoration" were changes in the kinds of men appointed to episcopal orders–especially in the countries considered to be hot beds of dissent.

In America, the Jadot era ended in 1980 when Archbishop (later Cardinal) Pio Laghi, a former nuncio to Argentina, replaced Archbishop Jadot as Apostolic Delegate. The new hierarchy included moderate to conservative clerics such as Bernard Law who was appointed to Boston, and former Rear Admiral John J. O'Connor, appointed to New York. Both men had reputations for being friendly and pastoral but also doctrinally orthodox. The humble and pastoral Joseph Bernardin, Archbishop of Cincinnati, was selected to head the troubled Archdiocese of Chicago. To other vacant Sees, Pope John Paul II appointed canonists, Roman-trained clerics and clerics with track records of having supported papal teaching in some critical areas: birth control, abortion, homosexuality and the ordination of women.

For a time, the conference of bishops continued the tradition of the 1970s and, under the leadership of Archbishops Bernardin and Rembert Weakland of Milwaukee, produced two very important pastorals. *The Challenge of Peace* (1982) and *Economic Justice for All* (1984) were drafted partially in response to the military buildup and laissez-faire economic policies of the Reagan administration. Put together after an extensive and complex process of consultation and several drafts, these publications challenged American Catholics to use the precepts of their faith to critically examine the public policies of their government. Eventually the authority and standing of episcopal conferences were questioned by Cardinal Ratzinger and other bishops, who protested the size and expense of the national bishops conference, some of them even wondering aloud why the conference issued so many statements on so many subjects. Others asserted their diocesan autonomy, insisting that any statement from the conference was subordinate to their own local teaching authority.

Knotty internal church issues were dispatched by the pope in very clear language. There was to be no dissent from official papal teaching on birth control–as enunciated by Pope Paul VI's 1968 encyclical *Humanae Vitae*. The ordination of women was firmly rejected as impossible since Christ himself did not do it. An updated catechism, suggested by American Cardinal Bernard Law, provided a new compendium of official Catholic teaching and a guide for orthodox catechetics. And a spunky Franciscan Sister of Perpetual Adoration from

■ *German Cardinal Joseph Ratzinger was appointed Prefect of the Congregation of the Doctrine of the Faith by Pope John Paul II. This influential prelate helped to set the tone of Catholic life during Pope John Paul's pontificate. He would succeed John Paul in April 2005.*
© Catholic News Service

Birmingham, Alabama named Angelica Rizzo, began a slow rise as an important media force in American Catholicism. This savvy nun had supported her Alabama convent by making and selling fishing lures and marketing homely little tracts with her homespun teaching. She somehow accumulated enough money to create a Catholic television network grandiloquently named the Eternal World Television Network (EWTN), and amazingly it flourished. She also carefully cultivated key officials in the Roman Curia who offered her protection and public support when her broadcasts and behavior sometimes offended. Throughout the 1980s and 1990s, Mother Angelica succeeded where others (including the Catholic bishops) had failed. Before the end of the century, the feisty nun had created a mini-media empire that rivaled televangelists like Pat Robertson, Jimmy Swaggart and Jim and Tammy Faye Bakker. Her brand of Catholicism was a mix of old fashioned catechism delivered in an endearing "Dutch Aunt" fashion. As time went on, her extemporaneous television shows became more querulous and hostile toward her perceived "liberal" enemies and even bishops and cardinals who crossed her. It was an incident at the World Youth Day in Colorado–a mimed Way of the Cross in which a woman portrayed Jesus–that caused her to erupt in a sputtering tirade on national television saying she was "sick" of liberals and declaring war on them. Her network broadcasts grew more confrontative and her stable of experts included sympathetic bishops and priests as well as conservative lay theologians from Steubenville and elsewhere who appeared at her side and treated her like the Queen Mother. The very idea that there could be theological debate over the meaning of sometimes complex church issues was considered tantamount to heresy by her network. Mother Angelica's influence over large sections of the American Catholic laity grew and her interpretation of Catholic teaching seemed to many to be "official." Occasionally she urged her listeners to report liturgical and doctrinal errors committed by priests and others–and provided the address of the appropriate Roman congregation where complaints could be lodged. Some of those letters found sympathetic ears in Rome. Her empire also included radio, a medium that had experienced a rebirth with the advent of opinionated talk shows. Her mixture of hard-edged doctrinal teaching, a hybrid Latin-English Mass, and pious devotions appealed to many Catholics stuck in long commutes or who kept the radio on as "white noise" in their homes or businesses. EWTN's televised broadcasts were carried into Colorado Springs homes via cable link-ups, which became more common in the 1990s. In 2006, EWTN radio broadcasts began on All Saints Day on KFEL, 970 AM with a signal that could be heard all over Colorado Springs and beyond. Mother Angelica and her co-workers, perhaps more than any bishop, changed the tenor and tone of Catholic life in the 1980s and 1990s.

In hindsight the 1980s and 1990s saw a gradual swing away from the mood and priorities of the 1970s. What became dominant was a concern for order, orthodoxy, a return to a more distinct identity for priests and nuns. To those who protested that this shift was undermining the spirit and letter of Vatican II, the reply came that many had misinterpreted the Council and that those in control now had a clearer and more authentic interpretation of the Council's meaning and intent. It was time for a "restoration" or a "reform of the reform."

Colorado Springs was of course very much in the middle of all this activity. When the Congregation for the Doctrine of the Faith withdrew the "imprimatur" from Anthony Wilhelm's popular compendium of Catholic teaching *Christ Among Us* in 1984, Vicar General John Slattery observed, "I was not only upset that a favorite book was declared to have fallen in disfavor, I was upset by the way it was done." But Slattery's unhappiness was not universal. He observed: "Imagine my surprise then when at the workshop on the RCIA [at the recent liturgical congress] one of the speakers stated his joy that the action had taken place."

Holding all this together was one of Bishop Hanifen's tasks. In 1985 after attending a symposium at Colorado College on "American Catholicism Since Vatican II," which highlighted presenters from across the ideological spectrum, Hanifen sounded a typically irenic note, "We need to hear each other, honor one another's viewpoints and reach out precisely where others don't see things our way. It's the only way the Church can grow in wisdom and maturity."

Colorado Springs Begins: Bringing the Church Together

Bishop Hanifen frankly admitted that he did not have a "plan" for the diocese apart from being its pastor. The diocese began with a culture of scarcity. Money and personnel would always be a problem. However, the smallness of the diocese and, despite its geographic diversity, its relative closeness to the See city were factors that provided grounds for hope. Hanifen initially placed a strong emphasis on education–especially adult formation. He hoped for ongoing formation for the clergy and expansion of opportunities for permanent deacons. For laity he hoped to network the lay education and forma-

tion going on at Benet Hill Center with the extension courses offered by Regis University and El Pomar Center, and by creating a partial tuition and grant fund.

Diocesan unity was to be fostered in a variety of ways. One of them was through the popular RENEW program imported from the Archdiocese of Newark and based on small group sharing during a series of planned sessions. Already in September 1983, the Archdiocese of Denver had adapted RENEW for its parishes and its kick-off event took place in Colorado Springs. The five seasons of the program stretched over a two and half year period with themes for each week of the seasons and parish-based discussion groups.

Congresses and workshops also provided opportunities for those involved in diocesan ministries to get to know one another and their bishop better. A diocesan liturgy conference, held in April 1984 at St. Mary's Cathedral had as its theme "The Ministry of the Assembly." Sulpician Father Eugene Walsh keynoted the event. In addition to general sessions, there were eleven breakout sessions, including one for priest-presiders directed by Father Walsh. Other sessions focused on scripture, sacrament and music. Liturgy congresses continued to be held at St. Mary's Cathedral each year, featuring a different keynote speaker and set of workshops. In 1988, these liturgical meetings seemed to be supplanted by a wider Diocesan Ministry Conference. The first was held at the Antlers Hotel and had as its main speaker New Ulm bishop Raymond A. Lucker who welcomed "Everyone doing ministry in the Church and...all people growing in their faith." In 1989, School Sister of Notre Dame Clare Fitzgerald keynoted the event with a stirring talk on the Church of the Third Millennium, "The Call and Cost of Discipleship." Eventually, the scope of the conference again broadened to include areas in the Mountain West and beyond. In 1992, Franciscan Father Richard Rohr keynoted an event that drew in 800 participants from all parts of the country.

Other groups in the diocese used the congress format to bring together their often diverse constituencies. Popular interest in the alleged apparitions of Mary at Medjugorje, Yugoslavia led to a conference in Pueblo in 1991 attended by 3,500 people and included talks by Bishops Hanifen and Arthur Tafoya as well as Jesuit Mitch Pacwa, a scripture scholar from Loyola University, and Father David Ricken, vocation director of Pueblo and future bishop of Cheyenne, Wyoming.

The Catholic press took a major step forward as well. For five years before the diocese was formed the Pikes Peak edition of the *Denver Catholic Register* covered local events. After a month hiatus, the new Colorado Springs newspaper, the *Catholic Herald*, rolled off the presses on September 5, 1984. Al Tucci, a retired executive of the Catholic Relief Services who lived in Colorado Springs gave the newspaper its name. The paper was edited and managed by the husband and wife team of John and Joanne Pearring. This faith-filled young couple had come to Colorado Springs from California to serve in youth ministry. Working out of their rehabbed old house in Manitou, they coordinated the formation of youth groups and published a series of well-received guides to youth group activities. Supplementing their income by writing for local newspapers and national magazines, they eventually hit on the idea of doing a Pikes Peak edition of the *Denver Catholic Register*, which won the support of editor Monsignor Charles Bert "Woody" Woodrich. The Pearrings formed a company, TextPros, LLC, which won the contract to publish the *Herald*. The paper, produced from their home, carried a compendium of local events together with press service stories that kept the Catholic community apprised of things happening near and far. They also found advertisers in the area and a niche in the local press establishment. In 1987, it became a monthly. Parish subscriptions, advertising, individual subscriptions and some diocesan support kept the periodical afloat.

A Feel for Catholic Life

The Pearrings were particularly good at highlighting stories from the various geographical regions and cultural groups of the diocese. In 1985 for example, John Pearring wrote one of many articles on the life of Catholics in the Plains, highlighting the successes of the RENEW program and stressing the closeness of parishioners in congregations like St. Augustine in Kit Carson and Sacred Heart in Cheyenne Wells, and touting area pastor Father James Halloran as a "new Padre of the Plains" following in the footsteps of the legendary Father Alphonse Keiffer.

■ *John and Joanne Pearring helped launch Catholic journalism in the Colorado Springs diocese. Their well-written and informative* Colorado Catholic Herald *helped create a sense of unity among the disparate regions of the See.*
© The Colorado Catholic Herald

A May 1989 profile of Kit Carson and Cheyenne Wells parishes introduced Catholic readers once again to these Catholic communities 140 miles east of Colorado Springs, where cattle ranches and wheat farms made up the meridian of life. Reliance on neighbors and community, avid following of high school sports, common concerns about drought and the condition of crops provided the backdrop for parish ministry. Special attention was paid to the priests and religious who worked in these rural areas. For example, Father Thomas Kihn, a former Oblate of Mary Immaculate had grown up a city boy and had a Roman education. When he was sent to a rural parish, he accepted the challenges of life on the plains philosophically. "I have to look at it in terms of ministry and calling.... I want to be where I am called to be." With no staff, comparatively few participants for such things as bible study and extra-liturgical events, Kihn understood that these parishes moved to a different tempo. Economic crisis stalked some of the rural areas as agribusiness transformed the face of farming. The inevitable shifts of economic life often removed basic services such as pharmacies, hospitals and department stores from areas—all of which had a ripple effect on local churches. Young people did not find jobs and moved to where they could.

New forms of economic sustenance took the place of the old ways of life. In Limon a state prison opened bringing people to work there. In Cripple Creek and Victor, casinos brought tourism and hotels and a clientele to the once thriving—then depressed—mining areas. What did remain was the goodness and generosity of the people who sometimes borrowed on their crops for diocesan appeals. Bishop Hanifen nostalgically recalled social visits to the region and noted the good humor and inspiring generosity of the people of these parishes.

Ethnic Diversity

Except for the Slovenian parish in Leadville (St. Joseph) and a Latino parish in Colorado Springs (Our Lady of Guadalupe), the new diocese did not have many nationality parishes such as existed in other parts of the United States. However, the area felt the same waves of demographic change that touched other parts of the American West. The growth of Asian communities, especially Koreans and Vietnamese, and the tremendous explosion of Spanish-speaking Catholics required pastoral response to keep these communities tied to the larger diocesan family.

The growing Korean Catholic community formed a parish in 1981, which met at St. Joseph's Church in Southgate. By 1995 they were able to break ground for a new church on five acres on Pikes Peak Avenue provided by the diocese. Bishop Hanifen and about 350 people attended the October 15th ceremony. By 1996 the original seventy families had grown to 130. The new church, named St. Andrew Kim, was completed in 1997. Unable to keep a pastor in place, the dedication was held off and the community was referred to as a "quasi-parish." The parish included Korean and English speakers—many of the latter American husbands of Korean brides. Children too generally spoke English. In September 1997, Jesuit Father Berchmans (Yong Woo) Lee arrived to shepherd the quasi-parish. Father Chul-Hyun (Michael) Kang later replaced him.

In July 1992 the diocese officially recognized the quasi-parochial status of Vietnamese Martyrs Church headed by Father Matthew Minh. Father Minh, a refugee from Vietnam, had come to Colorado Springs from New Orleans at the end of 1975 and early in 1976 had asked then Vicar Richard Hanifen for permission to establish a Vietnamese Catholic community. Beginning with a congregation of ninety, Minh gathered a group at St. Mary's Cathedral to which he ministered even when transferred to Our Lady of the Woods Parish in Woodland Park. In 1990 Hanifen appointed Minh to the full time pastorate of the Vietnamese Catholic Community. The community had its share of woes in finding a permanent location. In 2001 they moved four times within three months until finally parishioner Quan Van Nguyen and real estate broker Robert Carlone found a vacant church building on Wahsatch and Uintah Streets formerly owned by the Bountiful Blessing Church of God in Christ. The community finally had a permanent home, equipped with meeting halls, stained glass and a pipe organ.

The existence of the growing Spanish-speaking Catholic community was often covered on the pages of the *Herald*. The parish of Our Lady of Guadalupe began four years before formal foundation. In 1944 Spanish-speaking parishioners at St. Mary requested a bilingual priest for sermons, devotions and confessions. Father Emmanuel Sandoval, S. J., from Regis College in Denver came monthly to the Springs to minister to the Spanish-speaking. Theatine Father John Ordinas eventually took over for Father Sandoval. In 1948 the Archdiocese of Denver purchased an old Congregational church at 407 South Tejon, and the new Our Lady of Guadalupe Parish was born with Father Anthony Barcelo, C.R., as its pastor, celebrating the first Mass on September 19, 1948. Victory Noll Sisters taught catechism to the school children, and the structure served the community for thirty-one years. Theatine Father Francis Colom pastored the community from 1963-1969 and then returned in 1973 and was still serving as pastor when the vicariate and the new diocese were created. Father Colom was a beloved figure in the community, and one of several key priests whom Bishop Hanifen sought out for advice and support for the new vicariate and diocese. In his meetings with the vicar, Father Colom no doubt pointed out that the old structure was taxed to its limits as the number of Latinos/as grew in Colorado Springs, and the demand for spiritual and social services increased as well. "We were in a terrible state; we were getting desperate," recalled Father Colom in a retrospective. Then a parishioner noticed a "For Sale" sign on the property of East Side Church of Christ on Pikes Peak Avenue. "It seemed like an answer to our prayers," Colom recalled, "Here was a larger church building for a reasonable price." They purchased the property on April 16, 1979 and on December 16, 1979 the first Mass was celebrated in the new structure. The structure was modified to give it a mission look, and permanent deacons Emilio Reyes and Lee Sherpa served the community. An annual Guadalupe festival knit the community together, as did a mariachi choir. An effort to create a South American "communidad de base" Amigos in Fe was also tried. These groups and a host of other ministries turned the church into a thriving center of Spanish-speaking life.

Bishop Hanifen, who spoke Spanish, was eager to serve this growing community. In a gesture of recognition, he declared the Mexican national icon, Our Lady of Guadalupe, as the patroness of the diocese. At a 1992 Mass at the city auditorium attended by nearly 1,800 people—one of the largest events in the diocese's history—

■ *Deacon Lee Sherpa served for a time at Our Lady of Guadalupe Parish in Colorado Springs. He is pictured here with Bishop Hanifen*
© The Colorado Catholic Herald

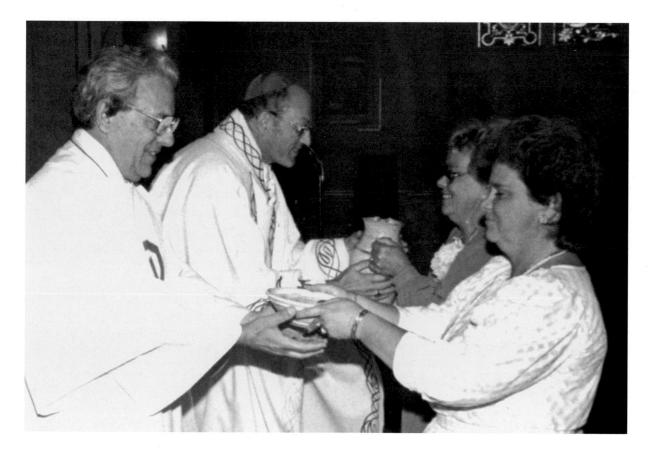

Bishop Hanifen apologized for the forced conversion of natives in Mexico and in the Americas. Hanifen prayed in English and Spanish to the Lady of Guadalupe before a life-sized painting done by local artist Gloria Hernan-Gomez.

Later that year, Father Francis Colom retired from his long pastorate and returned to his native Spain. Eventually, Spanish-speaking communities developed in other parishes, including St. Joseph in Southgate where Father Bill Martinez served as pastor in the early 1990s. Other priests who served the community included former Oblate priest Father Frank Quezada and Father Alfredo Garcia. In the early twenty-first century, concerns about immigration and the status of the undocumented began to move more prominently into state and national politics. Local priests and the bishops of Colorado worked hard to blunt some of the more negative and nativist expressions of the public debate and sought to ensure the human rights of those in the country.

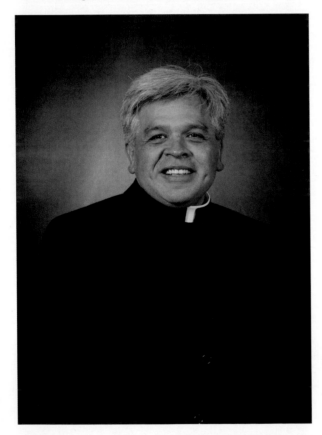

■ *Father Frank Quezada*
© The Colorado Catholic Herald

Priestly Ministry

The first edition (September 5, 1984) of the new *Catholic Herald* laid out a story that was to be a constant for much of the history of the Diocese of Colorado Springs: "Masses Cut Due to Priest Shortage." The unnamed bishops who fretted that the new diocese would not have enough priests were right. However, Bishop Hanifen saw it as an opportunity to work harder for vocations and also to further empower the service of the baptized to proclaim the gospel. Recruiting priests, nonetheless, was a challenge. At its outset, only twenty-seven diocesan priests and fifteen religious priests were available to serve the nearly 70,000 Catholics of the region. Fortunately, as Bishop Hanifen knew, the priests of Colorado Springs already enjoyed a spirit of fraternity reinforced by days of recollection, social events and mutual concern. Their interaction helped to blunt potential divisions common in other dioceses in the post-conciliar era. Most, in fact, shared memories of common seminary life in Denver and assignments elsewhere in the archdiocese. Bishop Hanifen endorsed the small support-group approach of the popular Jesus Caritas to help create presbyteral unity. Hanifen held four priests meetings a year to which all were required to come and which included periods of recreation. His approach to priests was collegial and non-threatening, governing primarily by persuasion, quipping that a mandate "created sixty percent compliance and forty percent saboteurs." Most priests appreciated his unaffected episcopal style. However, at one point his penchant for consultation and consensus-building hit a saturation point with some of the clergy, who insisted that he stop consulting and start deciding. The prelate claimed this mandate had "changed his style."

Bishop Hanifen noted in his early discussion of the priest shortage, "No ordinations to the priesthood are foreseen for at least four more years." He urged parish staffs and priests to strategize on the number of Masses that could be offered and asked Catholics to have patience, "We might not always find a convenient Mass available, but when we did gather for worship we could truly say: 'We have lifted our hearts to the Lord.'"

Hanifen relied on his knowledge of canon law to make pastoral provisions for parishes. He realized that not all priests were able to be pastors–either by choice or by temperament and that some lay persons were better equipped to serve in this capacity. With planning and the use of deacons and lay parish administrators, as well as the resourcefulness and patience of parishioners, Hanifen was able to cover most of the bases.

■ *Presbyteral unity is best expressed
at the annual Chrism Mass.*
© *Photo by Bill Howard,* The Colorado Catholic Herald

But the margin of error was always tight–an unexpected illness, a lawsuit or a call-back of a "borrowed" priest or religious by their bishop would leave him scrambling to fill the hole. Such was the case of three parishes in the Plains, which found themselves without regular services due to the lack of priests. Vicar General John Slattery crafted a schedule of rotation services, but acknowledged the long-term problem. "It's a phenomenon that we've been talking about for years and I don't think people realize the severity of this priest shortage. Every year it's going to get worse."

Initially, the diocese did not have the resources to appoint a full-time vocational recruiter, so those interested in the priesthood had to take the first step. Few seminarians applied to the diocese or persevered once they began. The first two for Colorado Springs were men in their thirties who came to the priesthood as a second career. The ordination of Ernest Bond to the diaconate and the installation of Robert Jaeger as an acolyte in April 1987 at Our Lady of Victory Parish in rural Limon, not St. Mary's Cathedral, was an early effort not only to celebrate their vocations, but to bring the oft-neglected rural church into the mainstream of diocesan life. On May 27, 1988 Bond prostrated himself before the altar at St. Mary's Cathedral and was ordained a priest–not only the first for Colorado Springs, but the first priestly ordination of Hanifen's fourteen year career as a bishop. Bond's ordination, however, did not offset the continual loss of priests. In late 1987 one priest resigned and three retired from active work. Nonetheless, a small stream of candidates continued to present themselves for Holy Orders. In 1990 William Carmody was ordained at Ave Maria in Parker, and in August that year Robert E. Jaeger was ordained at St. Mary's Cathedral.

Hanifen depended heavily on religious orders. The Jesuits have served at Sacred Heart Retreat House in Sedalia since 1959. Various Jesuit priests helped at diocesan parishes and for a short-time at Holy Family Parish in Security. The Oblates of Mary Immaculate pulled up stakes from the Manitou mission in 1984. This work was taken up by Holy Cross priests who also worked in parishes and sent help from their novitiate at Cascade. The Theatine Fathers pioneered the ministry to Spanish-speaking Catholics. Bishop Hanifen tried to recruit more religious orders, eventually bringing the Capuchins to serve in a storefront ministry.

Former religious order priests entered the ranks of the diocesan clergy by a canonical process called "incardination." Dominican Father John Krenzke and Oblate of Mary Immaculate Father Thomas Kihn were incardinated and assumed pastorates. Krenzke who was an associate at the large and thriving Divine Redeemer in Colorado Springs was sent to the pastorates of Burlington and Stratton. Kihn served on the Plains until illness sidelined him. Various priests from other dioceses came and went.

■ *Father Robert Jaeger (pictured here at center), one of the first ordinands of the young diocese, served often as a master of ceremonies for Bishop Hanifen.*
© The Colorado Catholic Herald

The Permanent Diaconate

Among the happy firsts of the new diocese was the ordination of Lee Sherpa to the permanent diaconate. Sherpa, a 65-year-old former trumpet player with Gene Krupa, Harry James, Glenn Miller and the Dorsey brothers, had experienced a mid-life conversion through the charismatic renewal. Sherpa and his colleague Leo Farrell began studies together in Denver's diaconal formation program. Sadly Farrell died before the ordination on September 22, 1984. Deacon Sherpa served at Our Lady of Guadalupe Parish until his retirement in 1992. Other deacons served in various parishes–occasionally administering them. Chuck Specht ordained to the Archdiocese of Denver in 1978 for service in the military ordinariate was another early deacon. Specht was a graduate of the Air Force Academy and spent twenty years in the service. After he retired in 1985, he served a semester as campus minister at St. Mary's High School and then took a full-time job at Corpus Christi Parish and later St. Francis of Assisi Parish. In 1984 Bishop

■ *Deacon Chuck Specht*
© The Colorado Catholic Herald

Hanifen appointed Deacon Specht as the diocese's first director of the permanent diaconate program. Subsequently, the number of permanent deacons and the scope of their responsibilities expanded as well. On May 27, 2006 Bishop Sheridan ordained thirteen men to the diaconate in a ceremony at Holy Apostles Church.

Religious sisters helped shepherd parishes for a time. One was Sister Rosemary Carraher who directed St. Francis of Assisi Parish. Lay women also stepped forward. In June 1987 Cathy Kredo was hired as a pastoral associate to manage the missions in Manitou Springs and Cascade. In fast-growing Douglas County diocesan mission coordinator Jeffrey Kelling gathered a group in the North Ridge elementary school gym on Sunday mornings for the beginnings of Pax Christi Parish. Five priests who took turns saying Mass in the gym that initially served the growing area, bounded by I-25 on the east, the mountains on the West, County Line Road on the north and Castle Rock on the south. Kelling was one of the first lay parish administrators in the Colorado Springs diocese. In 1992 Tom Shugrue of Denver was hired as the parish director for St. Francis of Assisi Parish, formerly guided by Deacon Chuck Specht. At one time six of the thirty-nine parishes were in the hands of lay people or deacons. But here too, financial issues had to be addressed.

Finance and Administration

One of the key players on Bishop Hanifen's team was Robert Doerfler. A 1976 graduate of Loyola College in Baltimore, Doerfler began his work in the Colorado Springs area after college by taking a youth ministry position at Divine Redeemer Parish. He became the first full-time youth director for the Southern Vicariate. In September 1980 he took on the job of business director for the parish and remained there until Bishop Hanifen appointed him to the Office of Administrative Services in May 1984. At that time, he assumed direction of the sometimes slender finances of the new Colorado Springs diocese. Finances were always a concern. The diocese received a "dowry" of $3 million when it was detached from Denver. But the gift came encumbered with demands. Of the $3 million endowment, $1 million was distributed in cash and $2 million in non-cash items, including $1.3 million in undeveloped land and a $650,000 note receivable from St. Mary's High School, and a $50,000 account receivable for a parish in Leadville. As it turned out, the undeveloped land was over valued and the debts from the high school and the parish were uncollectible. Of the $1 million cash, $150,000

■ *Robert Doerfler, chief financial officer of the Diocese of Colorado Springs*
© The Colorado Catholic Herald

was needed to provide relief to St. Mary's High School for fiscal year 1984. Another $50,000 was needed for working capital, $200,000 was set aside for plant and equipment startup costs, and $600,000 was set aside as a long-term reserve.

In an October 1984 report, Doerfler reported that the new diocese was only $4,950 short in its abbreviated first fiscal year, which ended in June 1984. He did note, however, that the 1985 budget needed more than $152,600 to meet its goals. A diocesan fund appeal, the Annual Diocesan Development Drive (ADDD) initially operated out of the Archdiocese of Denver. In 1985, the drive was renamed the Annual Diocesan Fund and was spearheaded out of the Colorado Springs office. Later it was renamed again and became the Annual Diocesan Ministry collection (ADM), which collected funds to run the basic services of the diocese–the Catholic Community and Youth Services, the proposed renovations of St. Mary's Cathedral and St. Mary's High School–and constituted close to half of the revenue the diocese needed for essential operations. In the meantime the diocese lived off the dowry given at the time of its severance from Denver. Assessments were raised on parishes, and by October 1985 Robert Doerfler reported an $80,000 surplus.

Doerfler, who had a number of financial responsibilities thrust upon him, relied heavily on assessments from parishes to keep the economic engines running. When five of them were unable to make their assessments in

1987, he must have had many sleepless nights. The annual drive made things a bit easier, and eventually gifts and bequests began to trickle in. But Colorado Springs was always on the edge financially. In 1992, shortfalls in the annual appeal caused the lay-off of four diocesan staff members.

The Chicago-based Catholic Church Extension Society was a major benefactor of the diocese, and in one very generous grant bestowed a $200,000 per year gift for five years on the infant diocese. By 1993 Extension had provided $1 million in grants–much of it poured into salaries for priests and religious to serve areas that could not support even a part-time minister, let alone catechetical programs, youth and campus ministries, pastoral planning or the education of priests and seminarians.

Administration

Doerfler's task was never easy, as the administrative costs of running the diocese consistently escalated. The first diocesan offices were housed in the old school building of St. Mary's Cathedral at 29 West Kiowa Street. The 1949-era building required some reconfiguring, but it served as headquarters until 2003 when the diocese purchased a nearby office complex on Cascade.

Bishop Hanifen tried to keep the diocesan staff "lean and mean," not only because of finances but also to allow as much to happen in the parishes as possible. However, as time went on studies of the diocese suggested that its increasing demands for services meant that the early structure was perhaps too lean and that existing staff were overworked. An avalanche of new bureaucratic work came when the Denver archdiocese

transferred responsibility for the education office, administration of employee benefit programs including priest and lay retirement programs, health insurance, property and liability insurance a bit ahead of schedule. The education component grew exponentially as Sister Jeanine Percy found herself supervising schools, catechists and lay ministers. Eventually three supervisors and two secretaries were hired to manage those tasks.

Hanifen himself was weighed down with administrative details and besieged by endless requests for his presence. To assist him in this he turned to his old friend

■ *Father John Slattery, pictured here as a young priest, was the founding pastor of St. Patrick's parish and a great help to Bishop Hanifen as Vicar General of the diocese.*
© *Photo taken from display at 50th Anniversary Celebration in 2007*

Father John Slattery whom he plucked from the pastorate of St. Patrick's Parish to serve full-time as Vicar General. It was Father Slattery's task to manage various duties, including filling slots left vacant by clergy. As time permitted, Slattery also took a hand in the various kinds of planning going on in the busy Colorado Springs chancery.

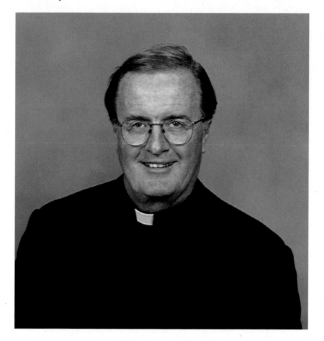

■ *Father Donald Dunn served as pastor of St. Patrick's, Vicar General and rector of the cathedral. A specialist in Catholic social services, he also played an important role in the missions in Colombia and Mexico.*
© The Colorado Catholic Herald

Father Donald Dunn replaced Father Slattery at St. Patrick and then later in the diocesan offices. Dunn, who took over the Vicar General's job in 1991 was also a friend of Bishop Hanifen and had come to the diocese in the late 1980s. Ordained in Rome in 1961, Father Dunn received a master's degree in Social Work from the Catholic University. He had served as director of Denver's Catholic Charities and Community Services from 1968-1980 and then from 1980-1983 as Vicar of Family Life and Youth Ministry Services. From 1984-1986 he served as a missionary in Monteria, Colombia. In Colorado Springs, Bishop Hanifen put him to work at St. Patrick and on the Priest's Personnel Board. As Vicar General, he oversaw priest personnel work. Bishop Hanifen was grateful for the help from these two close friends.

Efforts to keep up with the work were hampered by the lack of money to hire staff and do the kinds of programming envisioned by consultative boards like the Diocesan Pastoral Council. In 1986 the diocese invited Father Philip Murnion and Dr. Harry Fagan of the

Pastoral Life Institute to meet and assess the needs of the diocese. After interviewing the Diocesan Pastoral Council and the staff, the duo pointed out the obvious: diocesan leadership was both understaffed and underfunded because the diocese lacked money. It urged that the council should be disbanded, arguing that there was no sense planning for things until more money could be raised.

Over the course of his years, Bishop Hanifen was able to add staff and try different types of administrative configurations, which allowed the increasingly complex and demanding work of the diocese to go forward while he himself could move among the people and be a pastor. New employees assisted Doerfler in administering the temporalities of the diocese. Ongoing concerns for education led to the appointment of a series of educational coordinators to embrace not only the Catholic schools, but also the large numbers of youth in catechetical programs. Social welfare was almost an empire unto itself–with a diversity of programs to assist the needy and keep social justice issues on the table. Consultative bodies proliferated, with various boards and commissions dealing with such needs as worship, women's concerns and regional resource sharing.

Periodically new organizational charts were rolled out on the pages of the Catholic newspaper. In December 1999, seven key members of the bishop's administrative staff appeared on the front page of the *Catholic Herald*. Touting the reconfiguration for its "smoother and more effective functioning," Doerfler, who had been with the new diocese from the outset, offered the historical perspective: "Fifteen years ago when the diocese was formed, we didn't have a lot of rules because we didn't need them. Now we're fifteen, going on 16 years old and it's time to more clearly define and structure certain areas."

Finances remained a source of anxiety for the new diocese. As noted earlier, the financial demands of St. Mary's High School had consumed a substantial portion of the $3 million endowment given by the Denver Archdiocese. "We need to make the high school more efficient and less dependent on Diocesan funding," noted Bishop Hanifen in a February 1985 interview. The task would be arduous.

Agony, Death and Resurrection:
St. Mary's High School

The origins of the difficulties at St. Mary stretched back long before the diocese had been created. St. Mary's High School had been founded in 1885 and was operated by the Loretto Sisters. It was an institution of note in the community. Catholic educational affairs in Colorado Springs had for many years enjoyed a good deal of autonomy from central leadership in Denver. As we have seen, Colorado Springs had its own Catholic school board, which directed its affairs with comparatively little reference to the parent archdiocesan effort. This board had enhanced the revenues and enrollment of St. Mary by opening a popular extension course for young soldiers at Fort Carson who wished to earn their high school diplomas. St. Mary also had a satellite campus at Fort Carson (and another at Fort Lewis in Washington), and the government not only paid for the soldiers tuition but also sympathetic commanding officers gave them time off to study. This rivulet of funding allowed St. Mary to have a bus system, good salaries and low student tuition, thus providing economic stability to the high school for many years. Catholic parents became accustomed to the low tuition, but about 1983 a new commanding officer ended the time off for study for the Fort Carson soldiers. As a result soldier enrollments and tuition revenues plummeted.

Absent the income, the school began to run at a deficit—bridged over the years by subsidies from the archdiocese. By the time Colorado Springs was erected as a diocese, the school had more than $650,000 in debt—as noted, a liability wiped out by part of the $3 million dowry given by Archbishop Casey to the new See. Nonetheless, other problems surfaced. The school building was old; it lacked athletic facilities, and efforts to raise tuition hit parental opposition, resulting in downturns in enrollments. Bishop Hanifen continued to pour in money to help it make its bills. In an October 1986 bar graph in the *Herald* showing the allocation of ADDD funds, the high school's demands were the single largest expenditure—exceeding Catholic Community Services (charities) by $7,000.

The school did have a loyal core of followers who tried to shore up its shaky situation. Sister Jeannine Percy of the Office of Christian Formation, recognized the need to raise funds on a full-time basis. In January 1985 the highly-regarded Lt. Col. William J. Wallisch, who held a doctorate in education and had been an assistant to the superintendent of the Air Force Academy, was named president of St. Mary. Wallisch had retired from the Air Force Academy and pondered offers from

■ *St. Mary's High School, original site*
© *St. Mary's High School, Colorado Springs*

other universities. But he and his large family wanted to remain in Colorado Springs, and he felt strongly about the possibilities for the high school and believed he could help local residents see that "those who have enjoyed the fruits of education and our society need to pay back." His would be a challenging and frustrating task.

Wallisch assembled a board for fund-raising and development. By late 1985 he noted that there was a gap between the tuition charged ($1,600) and the actual cost per pupil ($3,000). Wallisch hoped for more enrollments and better public relations, and expressed his own belief in the school's programs and students. But he tried to remain realistic: "People may expect me to perform 'instant miracles' at St. Mary's. It won't happen. I'm just one guy with what I hope is a good plan. It takes time to undo decades of hard times.... We won't fix that with a band-aid overnight." At the end of 1985 he presented a five-year plan to increase enrollments from 328 to 500 students. The board asked that the diocese's $100,000 annual commitment be upped to $200,000 for this five-year period–after which it would drop back to $100,000 and then taper off altogether.

The plan did not work–but not for lack of effort. Occasionally ads were placed in the Catholic paper extolling the school and insisting that the Catholic community needed to support it. However, enrollments continued to flag–by the end of 1986 the student population had decreased to 268–creating even more acute financial difficulties. The solution proposed was more costly and even more financially precarious.

The school hired Peter Melcher, a member of the Independent School Management Institute, who concluded that the school desperately needed a new campus; it also needed more community support and involvement; and its tuition had to be raised. Wallisch and the board increased the tuition from $1,300 to $1,800, and the result was the feared decrease in population. What the board accentuated, however, was the need for a new high school campus, which would make the expenditure of such high tuition acceptable. One of the board members and developer John Venezia offered to donate a 26-acre parcel of land, located near Union Boulevard and Templeton Gap, valued at $1 million. Wallisch and the board challenged the community to raise the $3.5 million necessary to build and equip the school. If this was not accomplished, Wallisch warned that since the downtown location was no longer desirable, "it is inevitable that the shrinking size of the school will end up with the school not being able to open." But Wallisch's task

was difficult. Ninety-seven percent of Catholic parents in Colorado Springs sent their children to public schools.

Immediate reaction was mixed. Local pastors and Catholic school principals and even the superintendent of the rival public schools lamented the potential loss of the school and wondered why the Catholics of Colorado Springs could not support it. When reaction was solicited via a mail-in coupon in the January 7, 1987 edition of the Catholic Herald –the majority of those who responded supported a new school. However, a number preferred to see money put into religious education programs. Priests too privately expressed doubts that they could persuade their parishioners to contribute to a new school.

Hanifen kept abreast of the situation via reports from George Whalen, his school director. Both Whalen and Doerfler worried that if the diocese continued to support the school, it would seriously imperil other projects. By early February 1987 some of the diocesan priests informed Bishop Hanifen that the relocation plans were not going to work. Even when they stood in the pulpit and preached support for the faltering school, their parishioners did not respond. Summoning the priests to a meeting at the retreat house in Sedalia, Bishop Hanifen informed them that the school would close. Three of them, Fathers Owen McHugh, Jerry Kelleher and Thomas Kihn drafted a letter later sent to the parents of St. Mary students and reprinted in the Catholic Herald. It observed, "We have invested $1,848,205 over the past three and one half years just to support St. Mary's. Of this amount, $685,000 represents the debt incurred by the high school previous to 1984." With respect for the parents and the efforts already expended, the priests closed the door on any more donations.

On Tuesday, February 10 the school board was informed that the relocation plan was not working. The board then voted to close the 102-year-old school. Bishop Hanifen recalled that one of the board members, Leo Smendowski, left the meeting and apparently immediately began organizing opposition to the decision. It was planned to break the news to faculty and students on Thursday, February 12 and then to the public at large on Saturday, February 14. En route to the meeting with faculty, reporters–having already heard the rumors–besieged Hanifen who then moved up a press conference to the ominous Friday, the 13th.

Angry faculty and school parents blamed Bishop Hanifen for the closure. He had not directed his priests to preach about the school and refused to commit diocesan resources, earmarked for other projects. Hostile letters poured into the public and Catholic presses. One missive in the Herald attacked the bishop, "We know of your pre-occupation with your Colombian mission and adult education, but we never believed that you had so little regard for your own Catholic schools here in the Springs." The letter writers threatened to withhold contributions to diocesan campaigns and reduce weekly church offerings. Some insisted that the entire diocese had a moral obligation to underwrite the school and urged readers to complain to the Apostolic Pro-Nuncio, Pio Laghi. Hanifen stoutly defended himself, "I made a decision to go along with the majority of Catholics not to throw all our resources at St. Mary's. St. Mary's could not be considered in isolation from the rest of the ministries of the diocese." The head of the Office of Christian Formation, George Whalen, had the good fortune to be away at conferences in Denver and Kansas when the crisis hit. Interviewed by phone, he tried to make the best of the situation, but acknowledged, "There would be more blaming...and more to come for the bishop." Bishop Hanifen knew that he would be a target for a while—but mused philosophically, "The time to pick up the pieces will continue through May, and beyond. But life will go on."

On May 22, 1987 sixty-four St. Mary graduates walked across the stage to receive a diploma at the Pikes Peak Center and an era ended. However, those who supported the school could not be daunted. They formed a Committee for Catholic Secondary Education and hammered out a plan to use the existing St. Mary buildings for a nominal $50,000 rent in which they would operate a non-diocesan, privately-run Catholic school. Hanifen's financial advisors cautioned him against accepting this proposal, but the bishop nonetheless agreed to the proposition. He would give it another chance. The new school had challenges: renewing accreditation, recruiting faculty and raising funds–but with this literally new lease on life they resolved to keep forging ahead. St. Mary opened its doors for the 1987-1988 school year.

The results were not immediately positive. Enrollment did not go much higher than 200 students, and rent payments soon fell into arrears. In May of 1991 the Committee for Catholic Secondary Education offered several payment plans to satisfy its financial obligations to the diocese. However, it could not meet even its own payment schedule. Meetings between school officials and the diocese attempted to find a solution, but even though the indebtedness had been cut in half by

■ *New St. Mary's High School*
© *St. Mary's High School, Colorado Springs*

October they were still in serious default. In a special article to the *Herald*, Robert Doerfler explained, "St. Mary's has been in financial default to the diocese for many, many months.... We can no longer continue a financial relationship with the Catholic Committee for Secondary Education. We must look for options for the facility." Bishop Hanifen also rehearsed the troubled relationship in a *Herald* article, and tried to assure Catholics that he and the diocese had done everything they could. Resigning himself to a renewed wave of vituperation, he wrote plaintively, "We [the diocese] are not the enemy. We are friends. It is painful when we are pictured as anything less." Yet with the lease termination at the end of the academic year, the struggling high school still did not give up.

In 1992 the committee found a new building for the beleaguered school in the former Rocky Mountain Rehabilitation Center–the old Easter Seals building on East Yampa Street. This included 5.6 acres of surrounding property. That summer $200,000-250,000 was spent on renovations. In September classes began with a modest uptick in enrollments and the announcement of ambitious plans to build athletic facilities. The school then worked hard to plan for the future and to forget the bitterness of the past. Positive press in the *Catholic Herald* and a cooperative attitude with diocesan officials, such as school superintendents Sisters Jo Kassel, Judy Cauley and Evelina Bellfiore, kept the lines of communication open. Rhonda Miller, chair person of the St. Mary board, diligently worked toward reconciliation. These efforts eventually brought about the reinstatement of St. Mary as an official Catholic organization. As the millennium approached with the prospect of a year of reconciliation, Bishop Hanifen sought to heal some of the wounds. "When the Diocese was forced to give up ownership of St. Mary's High School, there was anger and misunderstanding. That was understandable and perhaps unavoidable in the face of such loss." On December 8, 1999 Bishop Hanifen celebrated a Mass in honor of the Immaculate Conception and formalized St. Mary's High School's official recognition as a Catholic school.

Engaging the Issues of the Day

Just as the diocese was being born, American Catholics were in the midst of a discussion on economic justice. Archbishop Rembert G. Weakland of Milwaukee had produced the draft of a major pastoral on the economy titled *Economic Justice for All*. The pastoral process involved submitting drafts to the public and the bishops and hearing the comments and critiques of those who had an interest in the matter. The text drew heavily from the social teachings of the church, including many of the addresses of Pope John Paul II and Vatican II related to this topic. It included a qualified critique of the laissez-faire capitalism that was making a comeback in the policies of the Reagan administration. Opponents of the pastoral, some of them Catholics, accused the bishops of advocating socialism when they insisted on the maintenance of a safety net of social programs and advocated policies that helped the poor and most vulnerable members of American society. Others simply dismissed the bishops as incompetent in the field of economics and argued that only business people lived in "the real world." Bishop Hanifen loyally presented the complex document to various constituencies in the diocese. In sometimes peppery question and answer sessions, he responded to critical questions from people who took issue with the document's diagnosis of the roots of poverty and its recommendations that the government do more to redistribute wealth in the country.

Another proposed pastoral, one on women, was in the initial stages of its consultative process as the discussion on the economic pastoral was winding down. Bishop Hanifen asked Sister of Charity Laetitia Slusser, director of religious education at St. Patrick's Parish, to put together a listening session on women's issues. Held in mid January 1986, the event included a questionnaire prepared to plumb issues related to the status and treatment of women in the male-led church. "There was great variety among us," noted Benedictine Sister Naomi Rosenberger, prioress of Benet Hill. All, however, lauded the opportunity to speak and have their voices heard. The Sisters eventually drafted a thoughtful discussion on the status and place of women in the local church. Nonetheless, the pastoral became so caught up in contention and opposition from the Vatican that it never was written. Bishop Hanifen did appoint a Women's Commission for the diocese, which kept alive the dialogue on the role of women in the church and surfaced issues of interest and concern, including domestic violence and gender discrimination.

In December 1982 Dominican Father Richard Woods spoke at a retreat on gay issues at the El Pomar Center. Afterwards an organized ministry to gay

■ *Athletic Field, Grace Center, St. Mary's High School*
© *St. Mary's High School, Colorado Springs*

and lesbian Catholics was launched in the area. In the spring of 1985 a local chapter of Dignity, an organization of gay and lesbian Catholics, formed. Its board met on several occasions with Bishop Hanifen. In 1991 gay and lesbian issues moved to the forefront when the city of Colorado Springs pondered removing sexual orientation as a category of discrimination. Some evangelical churches derided the protection as a "special status" for gay men and women and insisted that the bible condemned homosexuality. In response to these pressures, City Council members stripped the sexual orientation category from the list of civil rights protections. In a *Herald* column, Hanifen stepped into the fray: "Discrimination against homosexuals is wrong," he clearly asserted Catholic teaching on the immorality of homosexual acts, but noted, quoting a Roman document, "It is deplorable that homosexual persons have been and are the object of violent malice in speech or in action. Such treatment deserves condemnation from the Church's pastors wherever it occurs." The issue continued to be debated, and in May Denver voters left the words "sexual orientation" in the city's existing anti-discrimination ordinance–this despite the support of Archbishop J. Francis Stafford for removing the category. In the end, these two major Colorado cities took different approaches to gays and civil rights–Denver choosing to shield gays and lesbians from discriminatory practices while Colorado Springs did not.

In 1992 the issue was engaged on the state level when a ballot initiative, Amendment 2, that outlawed extending civil rights protection to gays was advanced and endorsed by the state's evangelical leaders. On June 5, 1992 members of the Colorado Catholic Conference, the church's lobbying arm, met at Colorado Springs with the three Colorado bishops, Hanifen, Tafoya and Stafford who decided to take no official position on the amendment. "Love the homosexual, hate the sin" was the shorthand for this difficult issue. Catholic positions reflected this divide.

The amendment won handily in the 1992 elections. In hindsight, Bishop Hanifen regretted the neutrality of their position. He had been taken aback by the media campaign of the amendment backers, which highlighted "fringe elements" (e.g., gay parades in San Francisco). These ads and the caricaturing of gay people were unjust to the mainstream gay populace "who are productive, caring and faithful." Bishop Hanifen, who had met many times with members of the local gay Catholic community, pledged to do so in the future and to continue "a pastoral relationship, because gays are our brothers and sisters."

Ecumenical Outreach

The homosexual issue was one that laid bare the differences between Catholics and their evangelical neighbors in Colorado Springs. Colorado Springs became an Evangelical Vatican in the 1980s and 1990s as major church organizations flocked to the city. One of the most prominent, Focus on the Family headed by popular radio personality James Dobson, came in 1990. Bishop Hanifen wrote a thoughtful editorial in the July 4, 1990 edition of the *Herald*, welcoming Dobson to town and offered to use the moment to open dialogue with these fast-growing ecclesial communities. Asking Catholics to move beyond a confrontational attitude based on differences in the interpretation of scripture–and the concerns of many evangelicals as to whether Catholics are really Christians–he urged, "We ought to be able to find ways to discuss our differences, and while respecting one another, continue to seek ways to resolve as much as possible those differences."

Not all shared Hanifen's sunny optimism about getting along with Dobson. A letter to the editor of the *Herald*, written by John McCormack, criticized Dobson's views on female submission, which advised men to be "enlightened despots to distribute carefully metered morsels of humanity to their wives, while admonishing women to assume a subservient role." He scored Dobson's advocacy of corporal punishment for children as "totally inappropriate for nurturing children to recognize people as inherently good, or encouraging children to develop a healthy self-image." Dobson and Hanifen remained friends over the years. The powerful evangelical leader, who advised presidents and whose favor was courted by prominent politicians, found time to attend a vespers service in 1996 to honor the 20th anniversary of the creation of the Southern Vicariate.

In mid-1992 another contentious issue surfaced, causing friction between evangelicals and their neighbors. Local rabbi Howard Hirsch of Temple Shalom, whose youth were being told they are not saved, contacted Bishop Hanifen who shared that Catholic children were hearing the same thing from the evangelical kids. Hanifen and Hirsch urged an amicable approach to this potentially explosive issue. They contacted Terry McGonigle of Young Life, a local evangelical youth organization, who agreed that something needed to be done. Together they invited many of the key pastors and local leaders to gather for lunch. These get-togethers became regular during the heated election season of 1992. "Their hope," McGonigle explained, "was that regular conversation over a meal might turn the tide of public rancor into a reasonable, faith-informed conversation...and points of difference could be discussed in a spirit of civility." By the spring of 1993, eighteen of them had entered into a "Covenant of Mutual Respect," which appeared on the pages of the April 4, 1993 edition of the Colorado Springs *Gazette Telegraph*. "The diversity of our religious perspectives may lead us into areas of possible disagreement," they wrote. "It is our hope to address those areas of difference with an attitude of openness, respect and love, and a willingness to listen and learn from each other, to the end that we may manifest the ministry of reconciliation." At a Diocesan Ministry Congress in October 1994, a panel consisting of those who had signed the covenant, Mary Lou Makepeace, a Methodist and city council member (and future mayor), Reverend Ted Haggard of New Life Church and Rabbi Howard Hirsch discussed the common need to "get along" and work for the common good. This collective effort to reach across the divide won the attention of journalist Bill Moyers who interviewed the participants for his popular public television series–even though he remained somewhat skeptical about its long-term impact. Nonetheless, the animosity between Catholics and evangelicals decreased significantly in Colorado Springs thanks to the face-to-face encounters encouraged by Bishop Hanifen.

Evidence of these warm feelings were on display in late 2006 when New Life Church pastor Ted Haggard was dismissed from his ministry after accusations of homosexual conduct. The widespread press coverage of the once powerful evangelical leader plunged his large congregation into grief and embarrassment. Catholic priests in the neighborhood, like Fathers William Carmody and Brad Noonan, offered words of support and prayers for the church and Haggard. Bishop Hanifen expressed concern for the fallen evangelist, his wife Gayle and his family, commenting, "I have known and worked with Pastor Ted Haggard for many years. I have always found him to be sincere, articulate in his faith and concerned for the welfare of the community."

Bishop Hanifen's friendship with Rabbi Hirsch and his commitment to ecumenism, continued to flourish. In 1995, Rabbi Hirsch founded the Center for Christian-Jewish Dialogue to continue the conversations begun in the controversies of the early 1990s. In 1998, this organization bestowed its inaugural "Dove of Peace Award" on Bishop Hanifen whose dedication to the cause of dialogue helped encourage better Jewish-Christian relations–a very important factor in a community so heavily dominated by Evangelicals.

Ministering to the Military

The concentration of military in and around Colorado Springs posed a special challenge to the diocese. The presence of military chaplains who provided sacraments and religious instructions satisfied in part the pastoral needs of the active duty personnel. Bishop Hanifen visited the bases, "as often or nearly as often as I do many of our civilian parishes," where he administered confirmation and conducted informal visits to deliver talks and hear concerns. A 1989 census revealed that there were 484 registered Catholics at Peterson Air Force Base; the Community Center Catholic Chapel at the Air Force Academy had 309 registered families–half living on base. The Catholic Cadet Chapel had 1,500 Catholic cadets out of a total of 4,401 at the school (34.9 per cent of its population). Hanifen urged local parishes to do a better job of accepting military families. Former Air Force vet Father Jerry Kelleher, summed up the situation: "Given the large numbers of active and retired military in this community, the church has a chance to make a difference, to make them feel welcome at their home away from home."

Perhaps the greatest challenge for Bishop Hanifen was the relationship between the military and the teachings of the Catholic Church –especially since the 1982 issuance of the pastoral *The Challenge of Peace*. The prelate spoke respectfully of the military presence and often cited his friendships with many in the armed forces. However, he made clear his opposition to the arms buildup of the Reagan administration although he insisted this did not mean he was anti-military. "I know quite a few people in military life who are also anti-war and anti-arms race," he commented. "I am hoping that military and civilians alike will increasingly address the frightening potential that the arms race presents us." Hanifen's boldest statement on the arms race came in April 1988 when he issued a comment on the Strategic Defense Initiative (SDI or Star Wars) of the Reagan administration. "The fact that our local economy depends, to some extent, upon the continuance of SDI efforts is not sufficient reason for concluding that it is of value to the world or our nation." At the summer meeting of the National Council of Catholic Bishops held in Collegeville that June, he spoke out again for critical scrutiny of the initiative. Other priests followed Bishop Hanifen's balanced but principled lead.

Father Owen McHugh of Divine Redeemer formed a Pax Christi group in his parish and was increasingly vocal from the pulpit in challenging the military buildup and speaking of the failure of the Reagan administration to use peaceful means to solve international disagreements. Religious women and others registered their discontent with United States foreign policy in Central America, particularly El Salvador. Popular opposition to the School of the Americas, a Fort Benning, Georgia-based training facility for special military units who sometimes murdered the innocent grew over time. A spectrum of opinions existed among Colorado Catholics, but many, Hanifen observed, "were very invested" in the Republican way of looking at things–including the military buildup.

Priests like Father McHugh occasionally found opponents who challenged their views even during sermons. When the Gulf War erupted in 1991, the questions arose as to whether this was a just war. Pope John Paul II expressed misgivings about the war, but these protests fell on deaf ears for many Catholics in the United States. Some local Catholics were interviewed in the aftermath of the war and were openly dismissive of any kind of restraint on U.S. actions.

Some Catholics felt conflicted about warfare and spoke out. But an even more vocal contingent was deeply opposed to the liberalized abortion laws in the United States. Pro-life activities in most American dioceses began in the aftermath of the 1973 Roe v. Wade decision. Father William Carmody, diocesan Respect Life director, became one of the leading voices in the local pro-life movement, encouraging prayer vigils, participation in the Life Chain–a pro-life demonstration that literally linked millions of pro-life activists across the nation–and speaking out for pro-life candidates while challenging others whom he believed needed to hear the message. In 1994, Father Carmody celebrated Mass in front of the Planned Parenthood Clinic. Pro-life demonstrators attempted to speak with women as they went into the clinic to offer alternative options.

The Monteria and Hermosillo Missions

The Diocese of Colorado Springs kept up its ties with Denver through its association with a mission project in Monteria, Colombia. Seven barrios or neighborhoods in Monteria, a city of nearly a quarter of a million two hours from the Carribean coast, had been a missionary outpost for the Colorado archdiocese since 1980. Father Thomas McCormick, "Padre Tom," founded the mission with the support and guidance of the Bethlehem Missionary Fathers who served in Denver and Colombia. Father Donald Dunn, later to minister in Colorado Springs, arrived after Father McCormick to serve the mission of Our Lady of Fatima, which had 80,000 Catholics.

In 1986 the mission welcomed Linda Romey as a lay missionary from Colorado Springs. Romey, the oldest of six children, grew up in Kansas City, Missouri and graduated from Jesuit-run Rockhurst College there. She had lived in Colorado Springs since 1981. A member of the Bijou House community, she had been a dedicated servant of the poor and peacemaking. In preparation for her work in Colombia she spent three intensive weeks in language studies at the Mexican American Cultural Center (MACC) in San Antonio. Her training took her into church statements issued by bishops of Latin America at Medellin and Puebla, scripture, liturgy and liberation theology. Once in Colombia Romey wrote back engaging letters that appeared monthly in the *Catholic Herald* –describing celebrations, lifestyle and the challenges of the area. In June of 1988, she sent a chilling account of the Easter Sunday murder of thirty-six campesinos by death squads– not forty-five minutes away in the town of La Mejor Esquina. Romey remained five years in the mission, returning home in 1991. Bishop Hanifen traveled to the mission annually after its first year–sometimes in company with by then Vicar General Dunn. In 1998 Hanifen announced that the three Colorado dioceses planned to return Our Lady of Fatima Parish to its local diocese and adopt a new mission endeavor in the Archdiocese of Hermosillo, Mexico. The tiny mission church of Santa Zita in Hermosillo was already being served by an American-born priest who also held down six mission chapels. Father Thomas McCormick was sent to represent the three dioceses in establishing the new mission field. At a packed Mass, Bishops Hanifen and Tafoya, with recently installed Archbishop Charles Chaput, OFM, Cap., in attendance, commissioned Father McCormick.

■ *Father Owen McHugh formed a Pax Christi chapter in Colorado Springs. His opposition to the military buildup of the 1980s earned him some criticism from local Catholics.*
© The Colorado Catholic Herald

Social Ministry

Until his departure in 1986, Tom Coterill oversaw the development of the Colorado Springs Catholic Community Services. After he left for a new job in Wyoming, Sister Lucille Krippel became executive director. The agency offered a steadily increasing variety of services to the people of the diocese: budget counseling, pregnancy counseling and adoption. It also had a Family and Youth Ministry office that worked with parishes and a Social Ministry office to provide food, rent assistance and visitation along with help paying utilities and transportation costs.

In 1986 the diocese helped underwrite Villa San Jose, a non-sectarian Housing and Urban Development (HUD)-subsidized apartment facility for those ages 62 and older with limited incomes. The genesis of this assistance began two or three days after the new diocese was created. Bishop Hanifen received a call from auxiliary Bishop George Evans of Denver telling him that HUD money was available for fifty units for the elderly in the Colorado Springs area. Bishop Hanifen turned to Franciscan Claudia Deats to shepherd the complex process. Similar HUD projects had been undertaken in Denver under Sister Mary Lucy Downey who oversaw $30 million for such projects in the Archdiocese of Denver. He helped her recruit a board under the leadership of John Armstrong. To secure "front money," Bishop Hanifen dedicated a portion of the annual diocesan fund drive to the project and facilitated the creation of a new housing corporation to receive the HUD funds.

After Villa San Jose was complete, HUD funding for another project, named Villa Santa Maria, came through in 1988. Directly next door to the Villa San Jose complex, this fifty-unit apartment facility went up rapidly thanks not only to the HUD grant and the diocese, but also to the El Pomar Foundation, which donated $300,000 for the $2 million project. A third project was on the drawingboard, but was never able to be built. Deats meanwhile built up an enormous amount of experience in the field of low-income housing that she later put to use in other projects in Colorado Springs.

A Bambino Bishop

Local concerns absorbed Bishop Hanifen, but the connection with Rome was never far away. The globetrotting Wojtyla papacy included visits to the United States in 1979 and 1987. Hanifen attended these events and told of his admiration for the stamina and resolve of the pontiff. In August 1988 in company with ten other bishops from Region XII, Bishop Hanifen made his first ad limina visit to Rome to report on the state of affairs of the 4-year-old Colorado Springs diocese. On the eve of the trip, he informed area Catholics that he would use his brief fifteen minutes with the pontiff to tell him that "the joy of starting a new diocese is the courage and generosity of the people of the parishes. I will share with him how heavily burdened the parishes are initially when they struggle to support a new diocese and how generosity is the hallmark of a successful start." At the papal summer residence at Castel Gandolfo John Paul II took Bishop Hanifen to his desk where he had a map of Colorado and put his finger on Colorado Springs. "This is your diocese," declared the pontiff. "Yes," replied Bishop Hanifen, and noted that it was "a bambino diocese." "Yes," remarked the pope, "And you are a bambino bishop!"

After a brief report, a pranzo with the pontiff and later a huge public audience, Bishop Hanifen followed the pontiff who worked the crowds after the audience. In addition to time with the Curial offices, Bishop Hanifen had a chance to meet with the American Ambassador to the Vatican whom the bishops were able to query about administration policy toward the Sandinista government of Nicaragua. A few years later, Pope John Paul II flew to Colorado to attend the World Youth Day celebrations at Cherry Creek State Park in August 1993. Bishop Hanifen joined the assembled bishops as did hundreds of Colorado Springs young people who greeted the aging pope with the enthusiasm reserved for rock stars.

In June 1992 Bishop Hanifen made a second visit to the Tomb of the Apostles Peter and Paul to report on developments since his previous visit. In the written statement submitted in advance, he reported the controversy concerning Amendment 2 and noted that his chief doctrinal problems came from "evangelical and literalist church groups in the community." Bishop Hanifen followed the President of Slovakia for his interview with the pontiff. In this window of time, Bishop Hanifen tried to explain what it was like to be a Catholic in a city with some fifty-three national or international evangelical Christian headquarters. When the pope asked what the word "headquarters" meant, Hanifen replied with its equivalent in Italian. He wrote that his visit to the various Vatican congregations was "more cordial and open to dialogue" than had been his experience in 1988.

One meeting that must have been interesting was with Cardinal Antonio Innocenti of the Ecclesia Dei commission in Rome—the body overseeing Pope John

Paul's permission for the celebration of the Tridentine Mass under specific need and circumstance. Bishop Hanifen's hand had been forced with this group when a priest named Anthony Ward established a Tridentine Mass chapel in Black Forest for Catholics who could not or would not accept the Vatican II Mass reforms. Father Ward, a break-away from schismatic Archbishop Marcel Lefebvre, was the founder of a group called Servants of the Holy Family. He had never sought Bishop Hanifen's permission to conduct such a ministry, but had appealed directly to Benedictine Cardinal Augustine Mayer, head of the Ecclesia Dei commission, which oversaw the expansion of the old Mass. Cardinal Mayer granted Ward official permission (a celebret) without consultation with Bishop Hanifen. In subsequent correspondence with Mayer, the permission was withdrawn. Hanifen met with Mayer's successor, Cardinal Innocenti in Rome, to discuss the matter.

In April 1992 Bishop Hanifen granted permission for the Tridentine Mass to be offered at St. Mary's Cathedral by Fathers Rawley Myers and Donald Dunn. In 1997, the Immaculate Conception Mission was established within the cathedral to minister to Catholics who attended the Latin mass. In 2000 Father Thomas Fritschen of the Priestly Fraternity of St. Peter began celebrating Mass with the community, and in 2001 Bishop Hanifen appointed him a parochial vicar at St. Mary's Cathedral with special care for the Immaculate Conception Mission. When the cathedral underwent renovations in 2002, the group moved to St. Joseph in Fountain and in 2004 Bishop Sheridan granted them independent mission status. In April 2006 a former Protestant church was purchased in Security and renovated. By 2006, the community counted 100 families from a range of backgrounds. On April 13, 2008, following Pope Benedict's Motu Proprio *Summorum Pontificum*, Bishop Sheridan elevated Immaculate Conception to a personal parish.

The Tenth Anniversary

As the Diocese headed into its tenth year, conditions in the American church were changing. Long-term modifications in the American hierarchy reflected the selection procedures of John Paul's papacy. Leading churchmen and EWTN placed a stronger emphasis on loyalty and obedience to the Holy See and the cessation of dissent. The publication of the English version of the new catechism in 1994 gave a sharper definition to teachings of the faith. Bishop Hanifen accepted all the changes loyally.

Within the church in the United States, the riptide of the sexual abuse crisis was building. Various cases around the country seemed to surface almost daily. The ever-building crescendo of depressing revelations about the scope and extent of the sexual abuse of minors created demands for accountability that would become progressively louder.

In the midst of all this, the diocese celebrated its tenth anniversary with a new pastoral plan. It restructured the diocese to meet the needs of its diverse regions and established, hopefully, a better sense of ownership of the diocese on the part of participants. Later the plan was refined to take into account the new catechism. Perhaps its most innovative and effective initiative was the creation of regional clusters presided over by a vicar. Veteran pastor Father Paul Wicker of Holy Apostles Parish drew extensively on the planning strategies of Robert Fritz and advanced a creative collaborative plan that divided the diocese into various sectors and created the structure for inter-parochial collaboration on a number of fronts including common liturgical celebrations as well as identifying and planning for new parochial growth.

Bishop Hanifen spoke positively of the future of Catholicism in the ten counties. "We will be continually searching for new ways for everyone to become involved in church life and service to the community in the name of the church." A two-hour Mass in late spring 1994 witnessed the installation of seven new vicars for the diocese. "What faces us," Hanifen shared with the people, "is a future based upon scarcity. We will face the scarcity of priests for the foreseeable future. We will continue to struggle with our limited material resources, despite the economic growth in our area."

■ *Father Thomas Fritschen of the Priestly Fraternity of St. Peter regularly celebrates the Tridentine Mass at the Immaculate Conception Parish.*
© *Photo by Jim Myers,* The Colorado Catholic Herald

In April Bishop Hanifen announced that he was taking off the rest of the year from May 1 to December 17 for a sabbatical. This idea had become increasingly popular with many American bishops. A few years before, Cheyenne bishop Joseph Hart had taken three months for rest, study and renewal. In Milwaukee, Archbishop Rembert Weakland took some time away to finish a long-delayed doctoral dissertation in musicology, while Archbishops Thomas Kelly, O.P., of Louisville and John Roach of Minneapolis checked into rehabilitation centers for chronic alcoholism. Bishop Hanifen made sure his flock knew that he was not fleeing or dealing with some hidden malady. "I am not exhausted or overworked. I am not discouraged. As a matter of fact I am one of the happiest bishops I know. I love you and our diocese." The trio of Fathers Don Dunn, John Slattery (rector of the Cathedral) and George Fagan, a diocesan canonist, took on the day-to-day affairs of the bustling Colorado See. Bishop Hanifen planned some structured study at the seminary in Denver, a month-long workshop in Rome, Spanish study at MACC, and various meetings and vacation and retreat time. He planned to return for the annual ministry Congress in October.

As he was preparing to go, Rome formally permitted the use of female servers–warmly welcomed by Bishop Hanifen but which simply ratified a practice long in existence in many parishes in the diocese. He also hurried up the diaconal ordination of Gus Stewart, a former Oblate of Mary Immaculate and a fairly recent "find" for the Colorado Springs diocese. In a hastily assembled ordination ceremony at St. Rose of Lima in Buena Vista, Stewart kept up Father Bond's precedent of being ordained in one of the diocesan parishes. On November 5, 1994 Stewart was ordained a priest at St. Mary's Cathedral. Three other priests were incardinated, Henry Smith and William Jarema both ordained for religious orders in 1983, and Patrick Battiato, ordained in 1976 for the Diocese of Trenton. These "new" priests helped at least for a time with the growing load of sacramental and administrative activities.

As Bishop Hanifen went off on his sabbatical, he could look back with some pride on what had been accomplished over ten years–and ponder what the future would bring for him and for the Catholic church in central Colorado. When he returned at the end of this brief hiatus, the problems and possibilities still remained– although by this time, the numbers of Catholics to be served were increasing even more rapidly.

Chapter 4

Growth and Transition
(1994-2002)

Bishop Hanifen returned from his sabbatical, full of enthusiasm for the challenges ahead. Much of the ordinary events of diocesan life marched on as usual. Awards were given annually to diocesan volunteers —the scouts and various others who gave unselfishly to the church (a lifeline in the often cash-strapped region). A steady stream of popular, nationally-known speakers came through the Springs —like Cardinal Joseph Bernardin, priest sociologist Andrew Greeley and Commonweal editor Margaret Steinfels. Each year the Rite of Election took place at St. Mary's Cathedral with a growing crop of candidates and catechumens preparing for the sacraments of initiation at Easter. In 1998 alone, 400 entered the church.

■ *Knights of Columbus Clergy Appreciation Dinner*
© The Colorado Catholic Herald

In Colorado Springs, homelessness continued its steady depressing ascent. Catholic Social Services agencies cared for the indigent. Sadly, even with their efforts and those of other church communities sixteen of the homeless died on the streets of Colorado Springs in 1994. Local advocates such as former Franciscan Sister Claudia Deats pushed hard to keep up with the need for shelter. Her Greccio Housing Unlimited, founded in 1990, provided low rent alternatives for limited income families. Deats had helped resettle Vietnamese refugees in 1975 and worked for Catholic Community Services in the 1980s to establish Villa San Jose and Villa Santa Maria. Operating on donations, federal assistance, grants and loans from the local community, as well as a local "Run for the Homeless," Greccio consisted of six properties by 1995 scattered throughout the city. Deats worked indefatigably to expand the amount of housing available to the poor and low-income dwellers of Colorado Springs. In 1998, her organization rehabilitated a dilapidated hotel on the city's west side. She also entered into a partnership with a California-based developer for affordable homes in the area.

Inspired by the Catholic Worker ideal of serving all those in need, regardless of income, Steve Handen formed the Bijou Community in the early 1970s. In 1986 Handen opened the Marian House Soup Kitchen in the old Loretto Convent on the Cathedral grounds. In 1994 Catholic Community Services took it over. The Soup Kitchen offered not only a meal but the only personal human contact many of the homeless received. Other services attached to the kitchen included a drop-in center, a small dispensary for basic medical care, shower facilities, a barbershop and other fundamental services.

The presence of the poor and mentally ill dramatically affected parishioners of St. Mary's Cathedral, located in such proximity to the Marian House Soup Kitchen. Some of the homeless used the cathedral's restrooms and slept on the pews. One person had committed suicide in front of the cathedral. In early 1996, 39-year-old Richard Dearsmith walked into the cathedral on Sunday, January 14, claimed he was Jesus Christ and tried to steal the collection. A struggle ensued with ushers as Dearsmith pulled an 11-inch hunting knife. Police tried to subdue the heavy-set man, and ultimately killed him in a cathedral bathroom. The event traumatized Mass goers and awakened some to the serious issues confronting the city.

A Changing U.S. Catholic Environment

By this time however, the mood and spirit of Catholic life in the United States had changed palpably. One locally explosive issue was the pastoral care for gays and lesbians. This drew the attention of Roman officials who launched a very public investigation of the New Way ministries of School Sister of Notre Dame (later a Sister of Loretto) Jeaninne Gramick and Salvatorian Father Robert Nugent. The duo had actually been under some fire since 1978, especially in the Archdiocese of Washington, D.C., where Cardinal Archbishop James Hickey had taken exception to their work and "soft" approach to the issue of homosexual acts as opposed to orientation.

Greater doctrinal clarity was assured when the long-awaited English edition of the Catechism of the Catholic Church began to appear in bookstores in June 1994. Structured around the articles of the creed, it encompassed lengthy sections on the sacraments, morality and an extended explanation of Christian prayer, "the raising of one's mind and heart to God or the requesting of good things from God." The Lord's Prayer was the focal point of this section.

The new militance of "orthodox" Catholicism found expression in a March 1995 conference sponsored by the locally-based St. Thomas Aquinas Society, which sought to reaffirm the traditional Catholic teaching that Jesus was really present in the Eucharist. The organization had been founded in 1991 by laywoman Therese Lorentz who had a dream about a prayer group that would be named for the famed thirteenth century theologian. From that prayer group emerged an organization that had the two-fold focus of prayer and education. The organization embraced St. Thomas Aquinas as its patron, because "he represents a straightforward approach to the Catholic faith." Private donations, fundraisers and hosted conferences featuring many popular speakers from EWTN funded the group. They also held annual priest appreciation banquets.

In response to a survey revealing that more than 50 percent of Roman Catholics believed that Jesus is only "symbolically" present in the Eucharist, the St. Thomas Aquinas Society organized a conference on the Eucharist in 1995. The host of speakers included Homiletic and Pastoral Review editor, Kenneth Baker, S.J., EWTN host Father Mitch Pacwa, S.J., Donna Steichen, Catholic journalist and critic of Catholic feminism, and Father Joseph Fessio, S.J., of the San Francisco-based Ignatius Press. Bishop Hanifen celebrated the Eucharist at its opening. Several hundred were in attendance at the Sheraton Springs Hotel to hear the various scholars and public figures. One of them, Father John Wishard, a converted Baptist and longtime Navy chaplain "with the voice of a drill sergeant," lamented the lack of reverence and manners on the part of the clergy, which diluted "the mystery that occurs on the altar." Father Wishard related how one pleasant afternoon in his chapel office, he placidly listened to a recording of Gregorian chant "pretending Vatican II never happened." The outspoken Father Fessio leveled a rebuke at the Diocese of Colorado Springs' liturgical vessels, "insisting that the pottery pieces were not worthy to be called chalices." He then turned the altar around and celebrated the Mass with his back to the congregation, offering communion under one species (refusing to pour the Precious Blood into the pottery communion cups). That the vessels had been used the day before by Bishop Hanifen added to the confusion. When asked about the incident, the local bishop charitably remarked, "Father Fessio evidently made a mistake in judgement." The society continued to host conferences, and their public visibility increased significantly when Bishop Michael Sheridan, Bishop Hanifen's successor took over the office in 2003.

On November 18, 1995 the Vatican issued a statement declaring that church teaching against women priests was "an infallibly taught part of the deposit of faith." Bishops in the United States fell loyally behind the proclamation, including Bishop Hanifen who noted that the decision "comes as no surprise." He was quick to remark, however, that "early reviews of the statement do not describe this as a formal ex-cathedra papal pronouncement," and he reached out to those in his own diocese whom he knew would be adversely affected by the ban. "For many I understand that the concern and possible confusion following upon the Congregation's statement causes difficulty and pain. It is a time of learning for us all. It is a time of patience for us all." Local reaction reflected a spectrum of opinions. Phyllis Hinsey, president of the Diocesan Council of Catholic Women, affirmed, "I agree with the Vatican statement. I think there are plenty of other positions for women in the church, for example homilies...." Sister Anne Stedman, prioress of Benet Hill Monastery, paid tribute to the "great gift John Paul II is to us" but spoke of her "great sadness" at the declaration "because of the gifts, I along with numberless others, have received from our holy mother church."

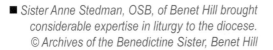

■ *Sister Anne Stedman, OSB, of Benet Hill brought considerable expertise in liturgy to the diocese.*
© Archives of the Benedictine Sister, Benet Hill

In 1996 Lincoln, Nebraska bishop Fabian Bruskewitz invoked Canon 1318 excommunicating various groups because of the serious scandal they gave by their activities. The list included traditionalist societies who rejected Vatican II as well as pro-euthanasia organizations like the Hemlock Society (which had moved its headquarters to Denver). Most controversially, it included the national Call to Action organization and its newly-formed Nebraska chapter. Bishop Hanifen, himself a trained canonist, differed with his brother bishop on the application of Canon 1318. While he acknowledged church disagreement with the Hemlock Society and Planned Parenthood on end of life and abortion, and that he found it hard to understand how Catholics could contribute to them, he did not believe that they should be excommunicated. "Controversy is not always criteria for excommunication." On the more knotty issue of Call to Action, he acknowledged that some of their positions were controversial, but that was an invitation to dialogue.

Challenges continued to abound in the area of public policy. Abortion remained a matter of grave urgency for local pro-life activists, especially during the Clinton presidency. President Bill Clinton reversed some of the modest pro-life actions of his Republican predecessors and on two occasions vetoed partial-birth abortion bills. Reversing Roe v. Wade became an even more urgent imperative of pro-life activists in every denomination. Annual commemorations of the January 22 decision mobilized support for legislative lobbying and public action. Physician assisted suicide, another anti-life trend sweeping the nation, was given an ominous boost in November 1994 when the state of Oregon narrowly approved a measure supporting it in a statewide initiative. The Colorado legislature introduced a similar amendment. This "Dignity in Death Act" drew a sharp rebuke from Colorado's bishops, and the lobbying efforts of the Colorado Catholic Conference were able to turn back the measure.

In Colorado Springs, complex questions related to medical moral ethics–birth control, capital punishment, the just war, abortion–all received fulsome treatment on the pages of the *Catholic Herald*. Columnists like Father Frank Pavone and Richard Doerflinger of the Secretariat for Pro-Life activities of the bishop's conference kept local Catholics aware of issues on the national level. Regular monitoring of Catholic interests in the Colorado legislature were also presented in the monthly paper. Likewise, public forums were held to discuss these issues–some in conjunction with Colorado College, which hosted lecture and discussion series highlighting featured experts in various fields.

Shifting the Emphasis on Church Support

In a major shift in its fund-raising operations, the diocese announced in late 1994 that it would move away from appeals and second collections to a total stewardship fund-raising concept. In a letter to Catholics in November, Bishop Hanifen declared Colorado Springs "a discipleship-stewardship diocese"–emphasizing the notion that all we have comes from God and that we are the stewards of time, talent and treasure. The proper return of these gifts to God comes from a conversion of heart and requires people to give based on their own sense of personal obligation and responsibility to return to God at least a portion of what He has given them. The practical result was the end of special collections, appeals and the like and a reliance on parish-based giving to meet the needs of the parishes and diocesan offices. "We look to see what we have received from God in terms of material things and seek to share what we have with those who need with sacrificial giving, giving that hurts in some way," explained Bishop Hanifen. Ten percent of parish income was to be pledged to the poor–with one percent of that going to diocesan appeals. Twenty percent of parish income would sustain diocesan ministries and 70 percent went to the parishes.

Ongoing Parish Growth

New resources would be needed. In July 1995 Bishop Hanifen observed that national statistics revealed that three of the ten fastest growing counties in Colorado, Douglas, El Paso and Park, were within the boundaries of the diocese. Douglas County was the fastest growing county in the entire nation. The diocese, which had begun with nearly 70,000 Catholics, now clocked in with nearly 80,000, mostly congregated in El Paso and Douglas counties. In January 1998 a new Metro North mission formed, and in July Bishop Hanifen appointed Father Gus Stewart as pastor. The mission became a quasi-parish, and the diocese purchased 17 acres on which to build its parish plant. By June 2000 St. Gabriel, as it was called, was granted full parochial status, and the bishop blessed a new church in 2004. In a unique confluence of names and theology a new mission in Elizabeth, called Our Lady of the Visitation, spun off of Ave Maria in Parker. Ground was broken for the

■ *Bishop Hanifen imposing hands*
on Bishop Samuel Aquila
© The Colorado Catholic Herald

Visitation mission building in April 1998. Longtime parish director Jeff Kelling left Pax Christi in 2000. In July, Father Ken Pryzbyla became the first resident pastor of Pax Christi. In the same issue of the *Herald* announcing Kelling's departure, another item noted the creation of a parish in the booming county with Father Larry Solan as founder. Catholics who abutted Denver were urged to join the new St. Mark's Parish in Highlands Ranch. Schools were in growing demand in the rapidly urbanizing areas of the diocese. In the fall of 2000, Ave Maria Parish in Parker opened a school.

■ *Father Kenneth Pryzbyla succeeded Jeff Kelling as the head of Pax Christi Parish.*
© The Colorado Catholic Herald

Cathedral Renovation

As new churches, many of them big enough to accommodate large crowds in the priest-deprived See, began to be built, the diocese turned its attention once more to St. Mary's Cathedral. The venerable old structure had undergone a major renovation when it was elevated to Cathedral status in 1984. In preparation for the millennium, it was decided to give the structure another makeover. Father Donald Dunn, now cathedral rector, spearheaded the lengthy project. He brought in liturgical consultant, Father Richard Vosko of the Diocese of Albany, to confer on the project. Father Vosko spoke about the kinds of symbols and space and the liturgical

principles required to undergird the project. Consultations began, and it was quickly determined that the renovation needed to provide a larger gathering space to "mingle and extend hospitality," to make each entrance handicap accessible so as to be a true doorway to faith, and to create a pleasing garden or green space around the church. Vosko recommended the retention of the basic architectural design and the stained-glass windows as treasures to be preserved. After considerable planning and rethinking, the project broke ground on May 19, 2002. The $7 million undertaking included long-needed repairs, handicap access, repair of the steeples and roof, and creation of outdoor gathering space. To help finance it, Bishop Hanifen sold the diocesan office building to Pikes Peak Community College. The project was completed in 2003 and rededicated in May of that year. Diocesan Catholics reveled in the new space and more comfortable worship areas.

■ *St. Mary's Cathedral underwent a substantial renovation in the early years of the 21st century. In one photo, the artists are restoring statuary. In the other shot, the cathedral center, a major addition to the existing structure, takes shape.*
© The Diocese of Colorado Spring

Priests for a New Millennium

Since the closure of St. Thomas Seminary by the Vincentians in 1995, diocesan seminarians attended the St. Paul Seminary in St. Paul, Minnesota. The *Herald* reported seven seminarians for Colorado Springs in 1996, including four–James Williams, Dan Ayers, Khan Pham Nguyen and Steven Parlet–scheduled for ordination in 1997, one of the diocese's largest classes. Father James Williams was dispatched to Rome for studies at the Angelicum. Jay Jensen, ordained in 2001, came to the Catholic church from a primitive fundamentalist sect known as the Assemblies of Christian Conventions where he had been ordained a minister in 1971. After a few years of living apart from denominational life, he was drawn into the Catholic church after service as a temporary organist. Leaving behind a career as a corporate travel consultant, Jensen entered Sacred Heart School of Theology in Hales Corners, Wisconsin as a student for Colorado Springs. Within a few years most of these newly ordained priests would be pastors in their own parishes. Alfredo Garcia had made his way to the diocese from Orratano, Mexico. One of ten children, he had begun his studies at Assumption Seminary in San Antonio in 1993. After taking some time away from clerical studies, he resumed his journey to the priesthood and was ordained to the diaconate in April 2002. In June Bishop Hanifen and a contingent from the diocese traveled to Mexico, where he ordained Garcia to the priesthood in an outdoor ceremony attended by the townspeople.

Religious order priests also continued to provide critical service to the diocese. In 2001 the Capuchin Franciscans from the Denver-based Mid-America province began a storefront ministry in the diocese. Five Capuchin priests, three of whom were bilingual, appeared at the Citadel Mall in Colorado Springs. Their center began in a former nail salon and then moved twice to larger quarters in the huge mall. Formally launched in November 2001 the Catholic Center was supported by the diocese and the Knights of Columbus. The little chapel welcomed 30-40 Mass attendees daily and a considerable number of confessions. The site of the brown habited Capuchin Franciscans took shoppers by surprise. One little lad walked up to the friars and said, "Jedis"–science fiction Star Wars knights. Assisting in local parishes and supported in part by the diocese, the friars opened friaries in the area and contributed sacramental services for the growing metropolitan population.

Still the demand for priests outstripped the supply. In a 2001 pastoral to the people, Bishop Hanifen

again brought home the severity of the shortage that had become part of the diocese's life. "It is unrealistic to expect," he wrote quite bluntly, "that substitute coverage for priests legitimately absent from their parish can be arranged on every occasion. Hence priests may be away for vacation, retreat, diocesan assignment, continuing education or emergency. On occasion, the parish may be without the celebration of Mass every Sunday." He noted, "We must together prepare for the reality of Sunday Celebrations in the Absence of a Priest." What followed were a series of instructions that defined both the reasonable expectations of priests in service and the key principles from the approved rite for Sunday Celebrations in Absence of a Priest that made provision for communities faced with priestless Sundays–including the formation of local teams to conduct Eucharistic services.

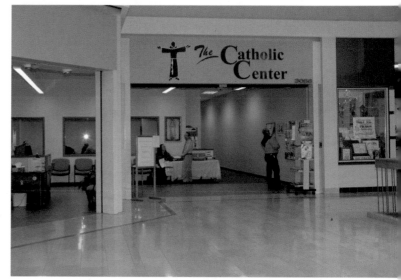

■ *The Catholic Center at the Citadel Mall is an important mission of the Capuchin Friars in the Diocese of Colorado Springs.*
© The Colorado Catholic Herald

The Hermosillo Mission

As new priests were welcomed to serve the flock, plans for a mission in Hermosillo, Mexico advanced with the commissioning of Denver priest Thomas McCormick who, as noted, had also served in the Monteria mission. All of the Colorado dioceses jointly sponsored the Hermosillo mission–as they had the one in Colombia. Father McCormick traveled to Mexico where he acclimated himself to Mexican life and language and then traveled to the mission where he met with Father Lance Bliven, the pastor of the parish. "I really feel at home," he wrote in his first dispatch to the Herald. "God's spirit is here, as well as there in Colorado, and to the ends of the earth." Care for the mission meant the sending of monetary and other kinds of resources from Colorado Springs. McCormick remained until 2001, aided by a steady flow of missioners from Colorado Springs.

At home the mission of charity continued to be advanced by an ever-growing social welfare network. By 1998 it had hired a full-time development director to underwrite its growing budget and was renamed Catholic Charities. Retired Air Force colonel Mark Dempsey spearheaded fund-raising until 2000 with a budget that had ballooned from $500,0000 to just over $2 million.

Heading Toward the Millennium

The transition into the new century offered another opportunity for the diocese to renew itself. Pope John Paul II had called for early Holy Year celebrations in 1984 and festivities in 1987 to honor Mary. In 2000 the traditional twenty-five year jubilee was called, and local celebrations took place. Colorado Springs folded in its particular celebration a year early when a confluence of anniversaries took place: the fifteenth year of the creation of the diocese, the twenty-fifth year of Hanifen's episcopal ministry and the fortieth year of his priestly ordination. Bishop Hanifen stated in a retrospective:

> When you look back to 1984 to see our new diocese you wonder how we made it. From a small vicariate of the Archdiocese of Denver we went overnight to a diocese serving ten counties of East Central Colorado from the upper Arkansas Valley to the Kansas border, from inside metro Denver to just outside Pueblo. We encompass the fastest growing county in the United States in Douglas County and several other counties in the diocese are fast on its heels.

With all this growth, Bishop Hanifen commented how much he "appreciated the pastoral care we have been able to continue despite the shortage of priests." He noted with happiness the success of the regionalization initiative and expressed satisfaction that the six regions were looking for ways to share slender resources and personnel. Pressing again for more vocations, he observed that the diocese had created seven new parishes or quasi-parishes without being forced to close any. All this had been possible not only with the help of religious order priests, but also lay persons and deacons.

While the diocese had its moment of concern about Y2K or a massive computer crash predicted as the millennium began, its real concerns were maintaining the viability of Catholic life and identity in the rapidly growing community. Millennial celebrations and growth also provided an opportune moment for capital fund-raising. Using the philanthropic consulting firm of Jerold Panas, Linzy & Partners of Chicago, long-term plans to raise money to meet the explosive development, especially in Douglas County, were laid before pastoral leaders. A 14-page document, "The Moment Has Come: The Vision for the New Millennium, The Catholic Diocese of Colorado Springs," revealed the need for at least seven additional churches, a new diocesan office and expansion of ministries such as vocations and educational institutions.

Eventually, the diocese hired the Fort Worth-based Cargill Associates to develop a five-year plan, the "Light the New Millennium Campaign." Although the professional fund-raisers urged setting a realistic goal of $9-12 million, diocesan planners decided to set the bar higher, hoping to bring in $21.5 million. The uses of the money were to build new churches, recruit vocations to the priesthood and develop Catholic education for people of all ages.

To advance the fund-raising, Bishop Hanifen organized a large Mass, attended by more than 3,000, at the Youth Outreach Center. The presence of Denver Broncos coach Mike Shanahan, whom Bishop Hanifen had recruited as the honorary chairman for the campaign, provided an additional sweetener. The progress of the ambitious campaign was slow, but by 2000 nearly 50 percent of its goal in the form of pledges had been achieved. By 2004 it became obvious that the $21.5 million target was unrealistic. By that time only half of the $10.5 million pledged had been collected. These monies, however, were quickly put to good use purchasing land for the new St. Mark's and St. Gabriel's parishes.

What with downturns in the local economy, appeals from parish-based drives and the successful building program at St. Mary's High School, the diocese continued to rely on parish assessments, the Annual Diocesan Ministry campaign and also transfusions of funds from wills, bequests, gifts and a subsidy from the Church Extension Society. The same story persisted–diocesan finances were precarious, reporting a $611,000 deficit in 2002.

A Transition in the Making

The tragic events of September 11, 2001 stung diocesan Catholics. At a noon Mass the next day, Bishop Hanifen addressed somber participants with a message of consolation but also warned against bitterness and vengeance. At the Mass and at a later interfaith prayer service, he drew upon the message of the epistle to the Colossians:

> See to it that no one captivates you with an empty, seductive philosophy.... What a challenge at this moment in our history when we are so victimized by those who genuinely hate us! We may, like so many others, want to fall into the empty, seductive philosophy of retribution. It is empty because it is never a solution. The decision to love our neighbor, even in the enemy, frees us from the sickness of perpetual victimhood.

■ *Bishop Hanifen is a well-respected figure in the American hierarchy.*
© The Colorado Catholic Herald

The end of 2001, a difficult year, closed on a high note for the Catholics of Colorado Springs. On December 4, Bishop Hanifen called a press conference for St. Mary's Cathedral at 11:00 a.m. where he announced that the diocese was to receive a coadjutor bishop in the person of Bishop Michael Sheridan, an auxiliary of the Archdiocese of St. Louis. Hanifen had turned seventy the previous June, and was technically five years from the required retirement age for bishops stipulated by canon law. "I was completely caught off guard by this," said Bishop Sheridan. Bishop Sheridan came promising to spend the time between his official placement and Bishop Hanifen's retirement learning about the Colorado See. He had only been to the Centennial State once before this hastily assembled December press conference, but Colorado would soon become his home.

Chapter 5

My Strength is Made Perfect in Weakness:
The Sheridan Years (2002–)

"I asked our Holy Father to send us a coadjutor," Bishop Hanifen wrote in early 2002, "so that the pastoral care of our diocese might carry on uninterrupted between my successor and me. In the wisdom of the Church, this has proven to be one of the best ways of transitioning from one bishop to the next.... My motivation in asking for this time of transition has been my love for you." Anxious to set aside the inevitable clerical handicapping during the changeover, Bishop Hanifen mentioned that his actual retirement and Bishop Sheridan's accession to the See would rely on "our collective wisdom to determine when the right time would be." That time would come almost a year after his arrival when the still-young diocese celebrated its anniversary of establishment. The Midwestern-born prelate would take the year to acquaint himself with his rapidly growing flock and adjust to life in the American West.

■ *Welcoming Bishop Michael Sheridan to Colorado Springs*
© The Colorado Catholic Herald

Michael J. Sheridan was born March 4, 1945 in St. Louis, Missouri, the son of John and Bernice Moore Sheridan. His father was a shoe-pattern maker and his mother a stay-at-home mom. "It was an idyllic '50s home," recalled his sister Susan Lockrem. "Our parents worked hard, but we never had much money." Baby-boomer Sheridan was a bright pupil. He attended Catholic grade school in Jennings, Missouri, St. Louis University High School and spent one year at the Jesuit-run Rockhurst College in Kansas City, Missouri. In 1964 his calling to the priesthood found a response, and he entered the archdiocesan seminary system and finished preparations for the priesthood in 1971. Sheridan impressed his professors and fellow students, and in 1974 the archdiocese sent him to Rome to study systematic theology at the Angelicum. His doctoral thesis was on Vatican II and the local church. "He was a child of firsts," his sister Susan noted. "The first in the family to graduate from high school, then college and then to become a priest." Calm, genial, unflappable in the face of setbacks and difficulties, Sheridan was also an amateur thespian. After completing his studies in Rome, he served as a parish priest and theological resource for the Archdiocese of St. Louis, writing editorials for the *St. Louis Review*. He also answered queries as a public spokesman for the St. Louis See. He even had an appearance on the popular Sally Jessy Rafael television show, an afternoon talk show. In 1997 Archbishop Justin Rigali consecrated him an auxiliary bishop and handed him the task of arranging the archdiocesan jubilee celebrations in 2000 and a 2001 Eucharistic Congress, which hosted 35,000 persons. He was officially welcomed to the Colorado Springs diocese at a Mass at the Antlers Hotel with 1,000 in attendance, including twenty-five bishops and Cardinal Roger Mahony of Los Angeles.

Bishop Sheridan experienced the normal pattern of joys and sorrows in working with his priests. The departure of Father Karl Useldinger from the active ministry in October 2005 brought a new chancellor and judicial vicar in the person of Peruvian-born Father Ricardo Coronado-Arrascue. Father Coronado took over both jobs in February 2006. Priests also supplied a strong measure of support when Bishop Sheridan's sister Susan died tragically in 2006. Father Donald Dunn celebrated a memorial Mass at the cathedral on February 2 with Bishop Hanifen preaching. One could only imagine the sadness that weighed on the heart of the bishop.

■ *Episcopal Ordination of Bishop Michael Sheridan,*
Cathedral St. Louis, St. Louis, Missouri
© *Photo by Richard Finke, reprinted with permission*
of Archives of the Archdiocese of St. Louis

The Sexual Abuse of Minors

Joy in priestly life was anything but evident as the clergy sex abuse scandal erupted again with a fury in 2002. Anger focused heavily on bishops who either ignored or misunderstood the nature of clerical sexual abuse of minors and transferred offenders from one parish to the next in the hopes of ending a problem. The national media ran seemingly endless stories of abuse and scandals involving clergy.

In Colorado Springs, the mood was tense, but fortunately the diocese did not have networks of clerical abusers as some of the larger Sees. Still, there were painful moments. Father James Klein, ordained a priest in 2002, recalled going to a shopping mall in Minneapolis wearing clerical attire and being accosted by a woman who yelled at him, "How many kids are you going to abuse today?" In June 2002, at a meeting in Dallas, the bishops agreed to remove permanently from ministry any priest who had abused even one minor. Bishop Hanifen had earlier been ahead of the curve on this issue, creating a Sexual Misconduct Investigation team early on in the life of the diocese. In response to the Dallas Charter, he created a diocesan review board, consisting of law enforcement officials, mental health workers and a parish. Ed Gaffney and Terri Sortor of the diocesan staff coordinated the response to this body. New policies included background checks on new priests, deacons and lay people associated with children. The bishop also appointed a coordinator for victim's assistance.

In early October 2003, the national bishops conference conducted an audit to see that the diocese was in compliance with the Dallas Charter and other policies produced to deal with the issue. Ed Gaffney and Terri Sortor worked diligently to produce all the materials and resources required. Colorado Springs "passed," and the programs and procedures intended to avert future occurrences became official diocesan policy. Awareness programs and other forms of education took place to make sure abuse did not happen again. In 2006 a lively debate erupted in the state legislature when a bill was introduced to remove the statute of limitations for criminal charges and filing civil actions for child sexual abuse. Opponents pointed out that the bill exempted institutions like public schools, which enjoyed "sovereign immunity." Abuse claims against schools had to be filed within 180 days and limited liability to $150,000. On January 31, 2006 the three bishops of Colorado and the Colorado Catholic Conference released a statement urging the House to put public institutions under the same rules.

■ *Edward Gaffney and Terri Sortor have played important roles in diocesan administration.*
© The Colorado Catholic Herald

By the time the sex abuse scandal hit with full fury, Bishop Sheridan was quietly making his way around the diocese, learning the human and physical geography of his new See. His year as coadjutor went quickly and at noon on January 30, 2003 Bishop Sheridan formally became Colorado Springs second bishop. Bishop Hanifen welcomed his successor and then took off for a six-month sabbatical to give him "breathing room." Bishop Sheridan noted, "The past year has been truly wonderful for me.... I cannot help but express my gratitude here, however, for the welcome that you have given me and for the many expressions of support and encouragement. Every priest–even the bishop–needs to know that he is appreciated and loved." Bishop Hanifen had earlier offered an astute observation of his successor soon after meeting with him. "Bishop Sheridan is going to be a decisive yet consultative leader." Sheridan would indeed bring a new focus to the role of bishop based on his perception of the needs of the diocese.

Sheridan Takes Over

At the end of March 2003 the diocesan staff and offices, as well as the Catholic Charities operation, moved out of the old St. Mary's grade school into new quarters at 228 North Cascade. The three-story, 30-year-old building was re-named the Catholic Pastoral Center and had ample room for the entire staff, the extensive charities operation, and even a few leftover tenants. The building cost the diocese $2.25 million.

Staff changes were inevitable. Bishop Hanifen's executive secretary, Mercy Sister Peg Maloney left her post for a position at Regis University. Peter Howard who had been working with the archdiocesan tribunal in Denver replaced her. Howard brought a well-defined theological background. He had received his undergraduate degree in theology from the Franciscan University of Steubenville and then gone on to receive a Licentiate in Sacred Theology from the Angelicum in Rome. Bishop Sheridan brought Howard on to do research and to help communicate the bishop's message and vision. "I'm excited," Howard told the *Herald*, "to represent the church in a time when there's a lot of confusion." In addition to his duties for Bishop Sheridan, he also wrote extensive articles in the *Catholic Herald* on such topics as the Terri Schiavo case and the morality of withdrawing feeding and hydration, Eucharistic Adoration, Mary's Assumption, St. Maximilian Kolbe, Marian devotion, the devotion to Divine Mercy and St. Faustina Kowalska (Sheridan inaugurated Divine Mercy Sunday celebrations in the diocese on the first Sunday after Easter) as

■ *The installation of Bishop Michael Sheridan*
© The Colorado Catholic Herald

well as other topics that drew very firm lines between right and wrong.

Bishop Sheridan revived the marriage and family life office in the diocese and appointed Christian and Christine Meert to assist couples preparing for marriage. Diocesan resources were developed for online materials that could be easily accessed at home. A diocesan Respect Life office officially began under Bishop Sheridan to coordinate pro-life education and events. Long held informally by Father William Carmody, the Respect Life gatherings encouraged occasions of prayer and action. Corpus Christi parishioners Joe and Peg Roach joined Father Carmody in this ministry. In celebration of the creation of the office, Bishop Sheridan celebrated a special memorial Mass for Terri Schiavo on March 31, 2006, the anniversary of her death. Meanwhile Robert Doerfler continued to serve as the Chief Financial Officer of the diocese, and Vincentian Father Mark Pranaitis was hired to head the Office of Stewardship and helped build the financial resources to allow the diocese to meet the demands of growth.

In 2005, a new pastoral plan was developed that laid out the key priorities of the diocese: faith formation, evangelization, social justice, stewardship and leadership development. Members of the diocesan administration assumed leadership roles in each of these areas.

Changes at the Catholic Herald

The leadership of the *Herald* changed as both of the Pearrings moved on to other jobs. A nationwide search surfaced University of Scranton graduate Bill Howard, the brother of Peter Howard, who had been serving as news editor for the *Texas Catholic* of the Diocese of Dallas. A native of Bordentown, New Jersey, Howard had earned his journalistic spurs first as a sports writer. "While I enjoyed sportswriting, my Catholic faith has always been my biggest interest and love." While serving on the staff of the *Texas Catholic* he had been sent to Europe to cover the death of Pope John Paul II. His reporting of the event won him awards. In addition to journalistic skills, Bill Howard brought technical know-how to create and sustain an online newspaper Web site for the paper. His enthusiasm for the teaching of Pope John Paul II had made him a founding member of the TOBET, Theology of the Body Evangelization Team, while he lived in Dallas. This group hosted regional and national conferences and study groups about Pope John Paul's theology of the body. Howard brought on new staff in Colorado Springs, altered the format of the paper and made it a bi-monthly affair. It featured articles by prominent Catholic writers and editorialists as well as local priests. The paper proclaimed its loyalty to the magisterium, quoted from Pope Benedict XVI, and used its columns to instruct the faithful in Catholic doctrine and a Catholic viewpoint about medical-moral issues, Natural Family Planning, Eucharistic adoration and issues such as immigration reform. In 2006 Bill Howard traveled to Bavaria to cover Pope Benedict's triumphal return to his native Germany. His reports provided interesting first-hand observations of the reception of the pontiff and his message.

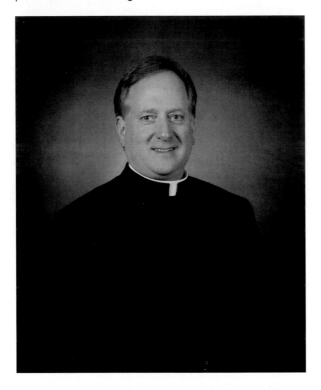

■ *Father Mark Pranaitis, C.M., Director of Stewardship and Bill Howard, editor of* The Colorado Catholic Herald
© The Colorado Catholic Herald

Father Frank Pavone, founder of Priests for Life, and an articulate foe of abortion also wrote regularly for the Colorado Springs *Catholic Herald*. The paper included Catholic apologist Patrick Madrid, ardent defender of Catholic teachings on such subjects as purgatory and the Real Presence. Madrid offered a Catholic way of interpreting the scriptures that came in handy when refuting the biblical arguments of militant evangelicals. In February 2005 Madrid traveled to Colorado Springs at the behest of the diocesan Department of Evangelization, and 240 people came to Holy Apostles Church to hear him lecture on apologetics and defend the Catholic faith.

The Iraq War

Notre Dame university theologian Father Richard McBrien's column was dropped from the paper and replaced with a column by neo-conservative George Weigel, a favorite of Pope John Paul II. Diocesan reaction to the outbreak of the Iraq War in March 2003 was mixed. Unlike the Gulf War coverage that highlighted the dissent of local activists and those opposed to the war, virtually no opposing voices were heard for Iraq, at least on the pages of the Catholic press. However, the ambiguity of the Vatican about the justification for preemptive war against Saddam Hussein and the reported opposition by the pope to the use of force to topple the Iraqi dictator, led Bishop Sheridan to take a cautious stance in the heavily military community. Urging support for the troops and the cause of the American forces, he stopped short of endorsing the war. Only columnist Weigel, who had been urging the invasion of Iraq since the late 1990s, was clearly in favor of the Bush administration policy.

Sheridan wrote lengthy articles for the *Catholic Herald* where he laid bare his considerable theological expertise. His early columns covered a series of disciplinary and doctrinal issues that he believed needed clarification. One of his first series concerned the recently issued General Instruction on the Roman Missal (GIRM), which was the "guidepost" for the correct celebration of the Eucharist. Sheridan's commentaries stressed the need for more reverence, silence at Mass, the need to genuflect and observe the Eucharistic fast. He called for confession before Mass and urged that tabernacles be placed in the center of the sanctuary or in chapels that were clearly recognized as reservation chapels. In his Lenten message of 2004, he wrote, "We live in a sensate culture, which is governed more by the ego than the will of God. In our materialistic western society we have become desensitized to the presence of evil because God has no place in the materialistic world." Bishop Sheridan's thoughtful and substantive columns challenged readers in many ways.

Bishop Sheridan's public support of the conferences of the St. Thomas Aquinas Society, which now enjoyed a measure of episcopal patronage not known under Bishop Hanifen, reinforced the emphasis on doctrinal clarity. These events grew larger and larger and were enhanced by popular musical and theatrical entertainments. Again, figures from EWTN dominated the line-up and included Johnnette Benkovic and Father Mitch Pacwa, S.J. The group brought other speakers who emphasized Eucharistic Adoration, highlighted their conversion to Catholicism from other denominations, or had founded contemporary religious orders dedicated to Adoration or pro-life activities.

■ *Father Ricardo Coronado-Arrascue, Chancellor and Judicial Vicar of the Diocese of Colorado Springs*
© The Colorado Catholic Herald

■ *The St. Thomas Aquinas Society sponsored a number of conferences for different age groups stressing Catholic identity and orthodoxy.*
Author Imaculee Ilibagiza signs books for attendees.
Pianist Eric Genius speaks with youth at a 2007 conference.
© The Colorado Catholic Herald

Bishop Sheridan's vision could not have been more lucid, and only those who did not follow his thoughts on the pages of the diocesan paper would be caught by surprise by his pastoral letter of May 2004, "On the Duties of Catholic Politicians and Voters." Here he put himself and the Diocese of Colorado Springs at ground zero of the emerging presidential campaign.

Catholics and the Politics of the 2004 Election

■ *Bishop Raymond Burke made headlines in 2004 by his insistence that he would not give Democratic presidential candidate John Kerry holy communion because of his stance on abortion.*
© Catholic News Service

Sheridan must have thought long and hard about his responsibility to provide his flock with clear guidelines to direct their voting especially where the subject of abortion and public policy came up. Other bishops such as William Weigand of Sacramento had publicly sanctioned pro-choice Catholic politicians; Bishop Raymond Burke of LaCrosse, soon to be transferred to Bishop Sheridan's home archdiocese of St. Louis, publicly stated his refusal to give pro-choice Democratic candidate John Kerry communion. Without endorsing a single candidate, which might have jeopardized the diocese's tax exempt status, Bishop Sheridan unmistakably asserted that Catholics had a solemn obligation to support candidates who upheld the right to life.

The Colorado Springs bishop took into account the "seamless garment" approach pioneered by earlier bishops, including Cardinal Joseph Bernardin of Chicago who asserted in a famous 1983 address at Fordham

University that the full spectrum of life issues should be considered in discerning for whom a Catholic may vote. However, Bishop Sheridan maintained that "not all issues are of equal gravity.... There is...one right that is 'inalienable' and that is the RIGHT TO LIFE. This is the FIRST right. This is the right that grounds all other human rights. This is the issue that trumps all other issues." He made it as clear as he could: "Any Catholic politician who advocates for abortion, for illicit stem cell research or for any form of euthanasia, ipso facto places themselves outside of full communion with the Church and so jeopardizes their salvation. Any Catholic who would vote for candidates who stand for abortion, illicit stem cell research or euthanasia suffers the same fateful consequences." Then came the challenging words that soon hit the airwaves, "It is for this reason that these Catholics, whether candidates for office or those who would vote for them, may not receive Holy Communion until they have recanted their position and been reconciled with God and the Church in the Sacrament of Penance." He went on to apply the same stricture to any candidate who embraced same-sex marriage. Although he did not actually say that he or any priest would refuse communion to anyone, his statement understandably was interpreted as such.

A press storm burst over the headquarters of the Colorado Springs diocese as hundreds of letters flowed in both praising and condemning the Colorado Springs bishop. Press interviews, talk shows and other outlets picked up on Bishop Sheridan's statements, and they became part of the polarized discussion within the church on these matters. The prelate weathered the accusations that his words would drive people out of the church and that they would not accept a bishop "telling them what to do." He remarked, "Let's be clear and honest. I have done nothing more than explain the teaching of the Church, which is the truth. If the truth causes people to abandon the greatest gift they will ever receive, viz., membership in Christ's Body the Church, I feel deeply sorry for them.... The truth of God can be divisive." In reply to those who protested that he was using the Eucharist as a weapon, he insisted that was not the purpose of his pastoral letter. But he did stoutly affirm that the reception of the Eucharist did have a relationship to the way a person lived. He knew that people did not accept this and commented, "This way of thinking comes as no surprise if we simply note the fact that everyone receives Holy Communion on Sunday and almost no one goes to confession."

In subsequent columns of the *Herald*, Sheridan took on the "thoughtful" questioners who challenged what they believed was his implicit rejection of the "seamless garment" approach. Why, they queried, weren't other life issues factored into the complex decision making required of conscientious Catholics? Was it possible that an anti-abortion candidate might have met the standards for defending human life at its inception, but have a perfectly abominable record when it came to other life issues such as capital punishment or endorsement of the Iraq war? To both these questions, Bishop Sheridan unflinchingly applied the principle that he had laid out in the pastoral letter: abortion, euthanasia and same-sex marriage were intrinsically evil and to be resisted at all times. Other issues were secondary. In fact, he suggested that prohibitions against capital punishment, despite Pope John Paul II's often vocal condemnation of the practice (including a famous episode in Bishop Sheridan's own Archdiocese of St. Louis when the pontiff secured the commutation of a death sentence of a condemned prisoner from Democratic governor Mel Carnahan), were not absolute. Sheridan himself opposed the death penalty and respected the right of Catholics to vote against anyone who endorsed it, but also acknowledged that the pope had never denied the "right" to execute prisoners deemed dangerous to public safety. Bishop Sheridan simply did not perceive any circumstance in which this right could be legitimately carried out and that there were other options short of execution to punish those who had offended. The refusal to declare capital punishment an "intrinsic evil" left a large gray area.

■ *Bishop Sheridan met the press often after his own declaration about politicians and the abortion issue. Here he is pictured with Pueblo bishop Arthur Tafoya discussing the moral issues of a local pollution problem.*
© *Photo by Bill Howard,* The Colorado Catholic Herald

On the subject of the Iraq war Sheridan acknowledged, "It is an issue that does not, in my opinion, allow for an easy solution." He carefully rehearsed the Catholic criteria for just war as found in the Catechism of the Catholic Church. When applied to the Iraq conflict, he recognized that "people of good will may disagree as to the moral legitimacy of this war or any war. This discernment always involves the possibility of error." But he insisted that "the evaluation of these conditions for moral legitimacy belongs to the prudential judgement of those who have responsibility for the common good." That of course meant the elected leaders of the country, who, according to lay theologian Michael Novak, an ardent defender of the war, had a special charism of discernment based upon their superior knowledge of classified information. Bishop Sheridan concluded, "Whatever judgements may be made by individuals concerning the decision to go to war with Iraq, we must remember that war, like capital punishment is not always and everywhere evil." Abortion, fetal stem cell research, euthanasia and same-sex marriage were objectively evil, "whereas a judgement about the moral legitimacy of war is a subjective one."

Other columns highlighted the official position of the bishops conference on the subject as well as a letter of then Cardinal Joseph Ratzinger, which seemed to support Bishop Sheridan's approach. When some commentators appeared to spin Cardinal Ratzinger's statement into a seeming approval of voting for pro-choice politicians based on other issues, Bishop Sheridan quickly remarked that other issues paled when compared with the deliberate destruction of innocent human life:

Is there a greater evil than the direct killing of a million and a half innocent human beings a year? Even the devastation of war does not come close to this horror.... What possible collection of goods could ever outweigh the destruction of human lives by legalized abortion? A stronger or more stable economy? Fixing Medicare? More jobs? An enlightened foreign policy? Not even the total elimination of poverty in our country could justify the direct murder of one human being.

Bishop Sheridan followed up his declarations by hosting four regional meetings on the duties of Catholic voters and politicians. Here local Catholics asked him if voting for a pro-choice politician would send a person to hell or require sacramental confession. The bishop carefully avoided making subjective judgements on the state of a person's soul, but insisted again and again that the slaughter of millions of unborn children required a strong moral stand by faithful Catholics. The assumption of many political commentators was that Bishop Sheridan's actions and those of other bishops who shared his approach really worked to the advantage of the Republican party. President George Bush opposed abortion, had limited federal support for fetal stem cell research, and even proposed a constitutional amendment to define marriage as the union of a man and a woman–this to underscore his opposition to same-sex marriage. Massachusetts senator and presidential candidate John Kerry, a Democrat and a Catholic, seemed to be under the stricture of bishops who did not threaten him with excommunication, but whose opposition to his policies were easily conflated with official Catholic sanctions. At their June meeting, Sheridan's brother bishops voted to leave the decision to give or withhold communion from Catholic politicians up to the local Ordinary. Other bishops kept silent when asked if they approved or condemned Sheridan's actions. Most acknowledged his right to teach and instruct as he saw fit in his diocese and to apply his interpretation of papal documents–they, the other bishops might choose other means to effect the same pro-life ends.

Bishop Sheridan did not of course publicly endorse any candidate. But his appearance and invocation at an October 12 rally with President Bush before 9,700 people at the World Arena in Colorado Springs may have sent an indirect message of support. Bush alone met Bishop Sheridan's criteria for a pro-life candidate. Bush's positions on the war and other "seamless garment" issues were secondary and subject to varying points of view–the prudent judgement of Catholic voters who could agree with the president in good conscience. Bush won the hotly contested election and the electoral votes of the state of Colorado. His standing among Catholic voters went up considerably, garnering a greater percentage of their votes than his Catholic opponent John Kerry. No doubt the misgivings Bishop Sheridan had expressed publicly and that were echoed regularly on the now popular EWTN network, concerning the senator from Massachusetts, had a decisive effect.

Another Pro-Life Issue

Bishop Sheridan did not flinch from taking on other issues, such as the death of Terri Schiavo, a disabled young woman in Florida whom some considered to be in a permanent vegetative state. This sad tragedy pitted Schiavo's husband, who wanted to end artificial nutrition and hydration, against her family who wanted to continue them. The situation gained extensive media coverage. Pro-life activists like Father Frank Pavone

and other Catholic religious made it a cause celebre for their efforts on behalf of the culture of life and against the culture of death elaborated in Pope John Paul II's encyclical *Evangelium Vitae* (1995). Politicians also became involved, delivering passionate speeches on one side or the other of the issue. When local court decisions favored Schiavo's husband, national politicians literally flew into the melee including President Bush who dramatically ended a family vacation to fly back to Washington to sign a bill pushed through Congress that curtailed local court jurisdiction over the matter. Terri Schiavo's husband eventually prevailed and hydration and nutrition ceased. When Terri Schiavo died, she was quickly cremated. Bishop Sheridan offered his sympathies to Schiavo's family after her death in 2005. "Terri's death represents a profound failure on the part of many people: her husband, the judiciary, and all who said or did nothing in the face of what has been a protracted act of murder. Another sad chapter in the annals of the culture of death has been written."

Tending to Growth

All was not electoral politics. The diocese continued to grow substantially and the need to accommodate the increasing demands on parishes and to build new ones accelerated–especially in Douglas and El Paso counties. The diocese turned 20-years-old in 2004, and in a retrospective Bishop Sheridan noted that there were more Catholics than ever and not enough parishes or Catholic schools to house them. Douglas County continued to develop with areas of El Paso County not far behind. In 2004 Ave Maria in Parker took the lead as the diocese's largest parish (2,400 registered households) with two Colorado Springs parishes, St. Patrick and Holy Apostles not far behind. The diocese devised a new master plan to cope with the growth to 2025, calling for four new parishes, three elementary schools and perhaps a central Catholic high school.

Funding the schools was always a problem as parishes found it increasingly difficult to shoulder the burden. In December 2004 the diocese formed Douglas County Catholic Schools, Inc. (DCCS), a nonprofit organization that would coordinate the fund-raising, land acquisition and other needs for future Catholic schools in that county. The diocese also hired Wisconsin-based Meitler Associates, a Catholic schools market analysis firm, to assess the viability of new Catholic schools and develop funding strategies for land acquisition and construction. In 2006 this organization moved to purchase land near Pax Christi Parish in Highlands Ranch to build an $25 million school. A capital campaign would raise the funds to build and also to pay back a diocesan loan for the land. The governance model was not tied to the parish but to the DCCS–an innovation in school organization. Ave Maria in Parker, the only Catholic school in Douglas County did not operate within this new structure but pondered joining it. Lines of accountability ran through the DCCS to the Superintendent of Schools in Colorado Springs.

A similar plan was advanced to assume control over the five El Paso County Catholic schools: Holy Trinity, Divine Redeemer, Corpus Christi, Pauline Memorial and St. Peter. Called the Unified Catholic Schools of the Pikes Peak Region, the entity transferred school funding from a parish-based to a diocesan-wide model. It created standardization for hiring, curriculum and accreditation. Scheduled to go into effect July 1, 2007 its first organizational reworking came with the closure of Holy Trinity School and its consolidation with Corpus Christi. Dwindling attendance, even with tuition assistance and other inducements, could not prop up the school, which had been in operation for thirty years. With the new governance structure, however, Catholic education could and would be available for those who wanted it–while a heavy financial burden was lifted from the shoulders of Holy Trinity Parish.

In his 2004 state of the diocese address, Bishop Sheridan declared, "Growth and expansion [are] still the name of the game." He then discussed parish development. The diocese had borrowed $15 million to underwrite needed expansions. Concerns for the poor continued. Catholic Charities managed to find a way to enlarge its Marian House Soup Kitchen–primarily by increasing seating from 75 to 150-175. It had been an arduous negotiation process with downtown merchants and neighborhood organizations, but details came together and the Colorado Springs Planning Department approved the necessary authorizations. In June 2006 a $5.8 million capital campaign was announced to build a new Marian House with an even larger dining room and facilities for the working poor and homeless who frequented it. The renovation and expansion of the facility was an occasion for Bishop Sheridan and Focus on the Family leader James Dobson to come together as the powerful evangelical ministry committed its support to the project. On May 23, 2007 ground was broken for the new Marian House complex.

Finding More Priests

One of Bishop Sheridan's boasts in his 2004 address was the appointment of a full-time vocation director. From the time of his introduction as coadjutor on January 30, 2002 Sheridan had identified priestly vocations as a key priority and promised to expend maximum effort to both model a joyful priestly life and also to personally encourage young people to serve the church. He celebrated the admission of young men into the seminary, and in 2004 found the resources to appoint Father James Williams as the first full-time director of vocations (even though Father Williams still had sacramental duties at St. Peter's Parish in Monument). Williams had earlier divided his vocational recruitment activities with the demands of his pastorate at St. Joseph in Southgate. "Everyone has a vocation," Williams declared, "it's a matter of finding it. God created us for a reason, and we have to turn to God for that direction." A vocation committee of committed priests joined Williams in finding new candidates for Colorado Springs and encouraging them along the way. The earlier formation of an active Serra Club in the diocese in the late summer of 2003 also aided Father Williams. Founded in 1935, this organization helped young men and women discern vocations to the priesthood and religious life. By the winter of 2006-2007 Williams was able to display the pictures of thirteen young men preparing for Holy Orders for the Diocese of Colorado Springs.

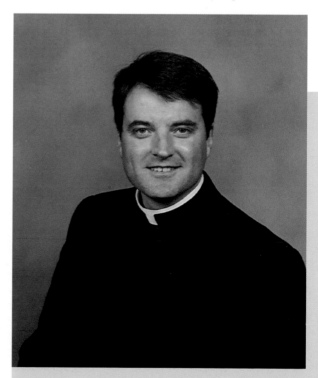

■ *Father Jim Williams, Vocation Director of the Diocese of Colorado Springs*
© The Colorado Catholic Herald

■ *Groundbreaking for the new Marian House*
© The Colorado Catholic Herald

A New Pontificate

Bishop Sheridan related his last meeting with Pope John Paul II, when he and Bishop Hanifen visited the clearly ailing pontiff in the late spring of 2004 for Bishop Sheridan's first ad limina visit. Here he had a chance to share with the pope the work being done in Colorado Springs vocations. "What a privilege it was to me to report that we have six men preparing for the priesthood, with several others expressing keen interest in entering the seminary." The following April Colorado Springs mourned the passing of the pontiff, who had authorized the establishment of their See. Bishop Sheridan eulogized him by remembering his first meeting with the pope at a special Mass in 1982 in the papal chapel with seminarians from St. Louis. "I came to know clearly and personally in that encounter that Pope John Paul loved prayer, loved the Eucharist, loved the Church, loved the priesthood and loved me as a son and brother." A relatively quick conclave elected Cardinal Joseph Ratzinger as the next occupant of the papal throne. The white-haired, kindly-faced theologian had for years been the enforcer of orthodoxy. Bishop Sheridan acknowledged the new pope's background, "No one in our day has

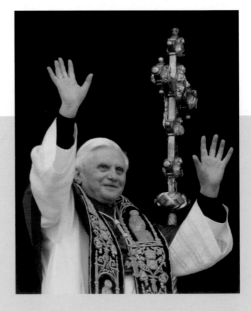

■ *Pope Benedict XVI, elected in April 2005*
© Catholic News Service

articulated the Catholic faith more clearly than Joseph Ratzinger. It is precisely because of this that some people–non-Catholics and Catholics alike are expressing reservations about the new pope, concerned that he is 'too conservative' or 'too rigid.'"

Spanish-speaking Growth

One issue on Bishop Sheridan's agenda was the tempest over immigration to the United States. A rising tide of anger and nativism, in part fueled by Colorado Republican Congressman Thomas Tancredo and television commentator Lou Dobbs, was being directed at Spanish-speaking immigrants to the United States. Many citizens, Catholic among them, opposed the violation of immigration laws and expressed concerns about the demand "illegals" placed on public services. The bishops of Colorado had appealed for generosity and balance in dealing with this issue, urging patience and justice.

Bishop Sheridan enhanced the visibility of ministry to Latinos/as by his appointment of Father Frank Quezada to the post of Vicar for Hispanics and to the rectorship of St. Mary's Cathedral when Father Donald Dunn retired in early 2007. The *Catholic Herald* had earlier begun to expand its Spanish language coverage and included translations of Bishop Sheridan's column as well as messages from Father Quezada. Editor Bill Howard soon began to receive what he termed "scathing" letters and voice mail from readers about the Spanish-language additions. "We are accused of encouraging illegal immigration and of encouraging Spanish-speaking immigrants to not learn English." Howard sought to reassure readers: "Regardless of what one thinks about the current state of issues like illegal immigration and border control, for the *Herald* to deny our Spanish-speaking brothers and sisters the words of God, particularly through our bishop, does only harm."

Conclusion

////////////////////////////

The Diocese of Colorado Springs will pass a major milestone when on January 30, 2009 it celebrates its twenty-fifth anniversary. Viewed from the perspective of an outsider, the history of the diocese reflects the history of American Catholic life. It was born in the mid-1970s, when the fires of Vatican II still burned bright. Its early leaders were anxious to create a viable and credible diocesan structure that made sense to the people in the unique social and geographical environment of the ten counties of the See. Even though hampered by a scarcity of money and full-time priests, the diocese moved forward to provide pastoral service. Some considered the formation of the diocese ill-advised or foolish. Those who dedicated their lives to it did not allow such skepticism to govern their efforts. While realistic minds and clear-thinking heads kept the diocese afloat financially and otherwise, the mission of preaching the gospel to its diverse constituencies remained an unalterable priority.

No one who actually reads this overview history could possibly think that this is all there is to the Diocese of Colorado Springs. At its core are people of faith who show up unreservedly to celebrate the dying and rising of Jesus each Sunday, who hope for a good education for their children and who donate their time and resources to make sure the gospel is preached. They are men and women who serve in the military, vacationers and tourists and those who serve them, miners, farmers and ranchers, and those who just fell in love with the scenic beauty of Colorado and would live nowhere else. Their lives are the fabric of the history that will be told when the diocese is 50- and 100-years-old. They daily ascend the mountain of the Lord.

Parishes

Ave Maria,
- Parker -

One of 13 missions administered by Monsignor John Judnic from Colorado Springs, Ave Maria's origins in Parker is shrouded with mystery because of the lack of records and data. Various priests served the Parker community, which includes Elbert, Kiowa, Elizabeth, Monument and Calhan as well as Ave Maria. The long distances and lack of available transportation meant that Mass was celebrated only once a month.

Along with the other missions, Ave Maria was closed in 1955; the altar, organ, statues and other church furnishings were auctioned in Castle Rock. St. Matthew Episcopal Mission moved the boarded-up church to its present location. It is still known as Ave Maria Chapel.

When Father Pat Valdez came to Parker in 1975 to celebrate Mass in private homes, attendance grew so quickly that Mass had to be moved to the Parker United Methodist Church. Established formally in 1976 as the Parker Catholic Mission, the congregation celebrated Mass at Joy Lutheran. Father Anthony McDaid became the mission's administrator that same year. To accommodate the growing number of parishioners, Mass was moved first to Pine Lane Elementary School (now Pine Lane Intermediate) and then to Parker Junior High.

In 1979 the mission's council approved the formation of a building fund for a permanent facility to be built by March 1983. Archbishop James Casey officially established Parker Catholic Mission as a parish and restored its former name, Ave Maria. Father Dennis Dwyer became the first pastor.

The first Mass in the new church was celebrated in 1984. Ave Maria, dedicated in 1985, became the first church dedicated in the new Diocese of Colorado Springs. Construction of a new evangelization center began in 2002, the same year the parish opened an elementary school. Spring 2008 saw the parish school's first eighth-grade graduation.

*T*he Capuchins moved to Colorado Springs in summer 2001 with Father Gene Emrisek, O.F.M., Cap., serving as director. With support of the Colorado Springs Diocese, the Knights of Columbus, and the Capuchin Province of Mid-America, they opened The Catholic Center — a 15-seat chapel — at the Citadel Mall on November 23. Bishop Richard Hanifen and Provincial Minister Father Michael Scully, O.F.M., Cap., each credits the other for thinking of the idea of opening a chapel in the shopping mall, and they credit Bob Taylor, the mall's senior property manager, for allowing the Center to open there.

Within the first year, the Capuchins expanded the project. They dedicated a 60-seat chapel with additional storage space and a place for meetings on its first anniversary. Father Curtis Carlson, O.F.M., Cap., became the new director. The Catholic Center moved to a temporary location in a corner during a renovation of its present space in 2005. The Capuchin Province of Mid-America took over the primary financial responsibility of the Center in September 2005; they dedicated the new Center space, a 75-seat chapel.

The Center's sacramental life has included the Eucharist, Reconciliation and Anointing of the Sick. The Capuchins work as pastoral counselors and also provide information for parish and diocesan events; the Center has become an invaluable community resource. The friars and volunteers have distributed Bibles, catechisms, rosaries and pamphlets and answered questions regarding the Catholic faith. Vocations to the priesthood and religious life have emerged and been nurtured at the Center. Numerous volunteers staff the Center, which is supported by benefactors who donate furniture, office and maintenance supplies, and financial resources. Other volunteers clean the Center free of charge and serve as sacristans, decorators, lectors and as Extraordinary Ministers of Holy Communion.

Holy Family
- Leadville -

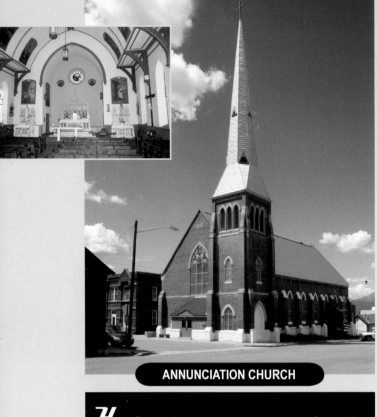

ANNUNCIATION CHURCH

ST. JOSEPH'S CHURCH

*H*oly Family is one parish consisting of two historic churches: the Church of the Annunciation founded in 1879 and St. Joseph, founded in 1899.

The Catholic population of Leadville is a community of faith and prayer. Daily Mass is offered with holy hour following. Once a month, on first Fridays, the Blessed Sacrament is exposed for an entire day of Adoration from 8:30 a.m. until 4 p.m., concluding with Benediction.

Four weekend Masses are celebrated, with one Mass being offered in Spanish. The Spanish Mass has recently started a children's choir. A prayer shawl ministry was inaugurated in September for the numerous elderly and infirm. This augments a very large ministry to the sick and homebound.

The parish certified three Spanish-speaking catechists in summer 2007. A vibrant youth group is active and religious education classes are offered in English and Spanish. The Confirmation preparation program includes a section titled "Theology of the Body for Teens".

As the demographics continue to change, with a growing Hispanic population, so do the needs of the parish. The parish has been exploring the feasibility of building a new Parish Life Center which would include classrooms, fellowship hall, commercial kitchen, offices and restrooms.

This parish exists in one of the least populated and poorest counties of the state. Challenged to preserve the faith, pass it on, and celebrate life in Christ now, the parish seeks to uphold community belonging and involvement as well as traditional family needs and values.

*F*ounded in 1916 from St. Mary's Parish and the missions in Palmer Lake, Modern Woodmen of America Sanitarium and the north end of Colorado Springs, Corpus Christi - the second parish to be established in the Diocese of Colorado Springs - served the area's English, Italian, Spanish and Slavic Catholics. Parishioners purchased and moved a Baptist church to the site of the present church and Fr. Felix Abel, the founding pastor, celebrated the first Mass in the new church in 1917. The cornerstone for the current church was laid in 1955.

The parish opened a school in 1921. It attained full accreditation by the North Central Association of Colleges and Schools. The school has a capacity for nearly five hundred students from pre-kindergarten through eighth grade. Its motto is "Be it known to all who enter here that Christ is the reason for the school".

Parish facilities have grown over the years to include five buildings totalling 76,000 square feet on one and one-half blocks in the Historical North End of Colorado Springs. More than 900 families support Catholic education and right to life activities. Parishioners have numerous opportunities to volunteer in church activities including youth, liturgical, catechical, musical, prayer network and social ministries. Parishioners also participate in various outreach ministries including BeFriender Ministry, visiting the homebound, sick, hospitalized and those in nursing homes. The Parish supports a food pantry, serves the homeless and sponsors a Christmas Giving Tree for needy children and families.

Several Ladies Circles assist those in need in the parish and community, and the Wednesday Warriors volunteer to maintain parish facilities. The Parish Hall, available to a wide variety of groups, supports fellowship, social and community activities.

Corpus Christi has been served by the following Pastors:

Fr. Felix Abel .... 1916 - 1941
Fr. Anthony Elzi .... 1941 - 1972
Fr. Robert Kekeisen .... 1972 - 1985
Fr. Gerald H. Bruggeman .... 1985 - 1994
Fr. Bill Carmody .... 1994 - 2000
Fr. Donald Dunn .... Jan - Jun 2000
Fr. John Slattery .... Jul - Dec 2000
Fr. Steve Parlet .... Jan 2001 - Jun 2007
Fr. Mark Zacker .... Jul 2007 - Present

Divine Redeemer,
– Colorado Springs –

*B*ishop Urban J. Vehr saw the spiritual need of Catholics in the eastern sections of Colorado Springs, and in 1947 the Archdiocese of Denver purchased property for what is now Divine Redeemer. Father Theobold was appointed pastor in 1950. Mass was first celebrated at St. Francis Hospital Chapel, then, with the help of Senator Edwin Johnson, at the abandoned Officers Club of Ent Air Force Base. The first Mass was offered there on Aug. 13, 1950, and it served as a temporary worship space until a church was constructed and dedicated in 1951. A census taken at this time indicated that 250 Catholic families lived within the parish boundaries.

The thriving parish constructed a new church-and-school building in 1956. The 25,000-square-foot structure cost $212,000. The Sisters of Charity of Cincinnati — Sisters Jean Therese, Rosina and Ann Rafael, led by Sister Francis Assisium — oversaw the school. They lived temporarily at the Clockner Penrose Hospital while a convent was being built. Eight additional classrooms were added by September 1957, enabling the building to accommodate an enrollment of 800 students. A convent and a rectory were constructed that year.

When the parish membership reached 1,200 families, the community required a larger worship space. After many months of meetings, planning, and reviews,

parishioners selected an architect, and the construction of a new church began in 1969. The new Divine Redeemer was dedicated in December 1970. The parish became part of the Colorado Springs Diocese in 1984.

The parish — now more than 50 years old — continues to serve the community. The school is again growing, with more than 325 students in kindergarten through grade eight. Parish programs both enrich spiritual needs and address temporal ones such as organizing a food pantry that serves all of Colorado Springs.

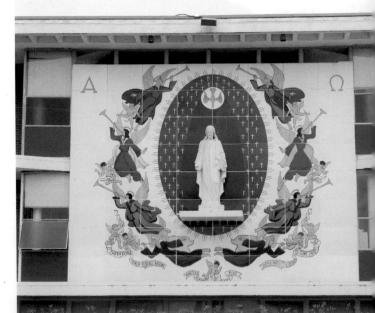

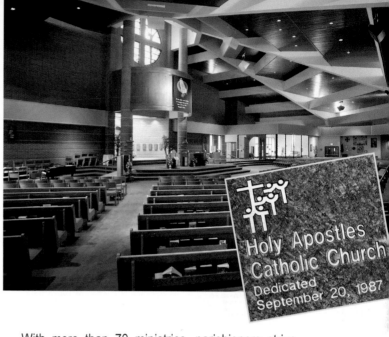

Holy Apostles Catholic Church Dedicated September 20, 1987

$\mathcal{E}$stablished in 1972 by father Wicker with only 13 families, Holy Apostles served the growing Catholic population in the northeast section of Colorado Springs. It attained parish status in 1973. Plans for a new church building were underway almost immediately, and a new church was dedicated in 1974 and included a parent-cooperative preschool program. By 1978 more than 750 families belonged to the parish, and by 1984 more than 1,200 families worshipped at the church, causing the parish to outgrow the structure. A new church — the largest Catholic worship space in Colorado Springs — , was constructed in 1987. Today the parish has more than 2,300 registered families. Father Wicker is still in charge of the parish.

A diverse congregation, parishioners celebrate and share ethnic traditions, including the Sicilian St. Joseph's Table, the Portuguese celebration of St. Isabella and the Hispanic celebration of Our Lady of Guadalupe. The parish hosts an annual festival, first organized in 1991, that is part of its outreach to the local community. The preschool, still operating in the church, achieved and maintained full accreditation by the National Association for the Education of Young Children.

With more than 70 ministries, parishioners strive to make an impact in the community. Each parishioner serves as an agent of hope. Holy Apostles emphasizes religious education for adults and children, supports a charismatic prayer group and participates in numerous outreach service activities that comfort the grieving and aid those in crisis. The parish hosts a Super Bowl party for the homeless and provides 800 families with Thanksgiving dinners and Christmas gifts. Holy Apostles is also a member of Northern Churches Care, an ecumenical group providing food and financial assistance to the city's needy. The parish took the lead in raising more than $250,000 for the new Marian House Soup Kitchen.

Holy Family,
- Security -

*E*stablished in 1957 as part of the Denver Diocese with Father Joseph Leberer as the founding pastor, Holy Family served Catholics within the southern limits of Colorado Springs. Mass was first celebrated at the Remple Memorial Chapel, a mortuary chapel now called New Hope in the Rockies. Mass was also celebrated at Widefield High School. Parishioners immediately purchased a rectory, formed an altar and rosary society, organized a capital campaign for a new church, and broke ground that same year.

In a building designed primarily as a gymnasium, with the hope of building a new church later, three Masses were celebrated on Easter Sunday 1958. The dedication occurred in December. Parishioners established a council of the Knights of Columbus in 1958 and a court for the Catholic Daughters of the Americas in 1959. In later years the Legion of Mary was invited to form a group whose members to this day continue to lead the rosary before Mass. The Knights built their own hall and there they continue to meet.

An education center was built in 1967, and in 1968, a new rectory; the former rectory became a convent. Two Maryknoll Sisters had formed religious education classes before the parish was established, a program that was expanded in 1968 and coordinated by Sister Ruth Vontz. Sister Ann became director in 1979, serving until her death in 1982.

The convent was sold in 1972, and the church's interior was remodeled to its present design in 1975. The parish made history when it established the first Perpetual Adoration chapel in the Colorado Springs Diocese — named the Precious Blood of Jesus Chapel — dedicated in 1994.

*F*rank Cusack built Holy Rosary Chapel in 1931 as a memorial to his parents, Thomas and Mary Green Cusack, and deeded it and the property that same year to the Diocese of Denver. A beautiful, quaint edifice on a hilltop overlooking Cascade, the chapel is built of stones — local red rock — from Pyramid Mountain; the red cut-stone trim came from the quarry at the end of Ute Pass.

Archbishop Urban J. Vehr of Denver celebrated the first Mass in the chapel in July 1931, dedicating it as the Chapel of the Holy Rosary as at Lourdes. A grotto shrine to Our Lady of Lourdes is located underneath the chapel, accessible by an iron staircase from the vestibule. The chapel, sought after for weddings, serves Catholics in Cascade, Chipita Park and Green Mountain Falls and is a popular worship place for summer visitors.

European artists designed and fashioned the chapel's appointments: Franz Mayer Studios of Munich designed the five stained-glass windows that depict the 15 mysteries of the Rosary on three different levels, the Stations of the Cross in vibrantly colored semi-mosaic glass on bronze, and the window-sized mosaic over the sacristy door that shows St. Dominic receiving the Rosary from the Blessed Virgin.

A life-sized crucifix representing Christ the King hangs above the altar, beneath a marble replica of the Last Supper by Italian artist Lualdi. A small balcony houses a two-manual Kilgen pipe organ under a stained-glass rose window dedicated to St. Cecilia, patron saint of music, to whom the Cusack children were devoted.

A 1998 renovation — dedicated that November — replaced the priest's quarters with an enlarged meeting room and kitchen facility for parish gatherings. Parishioners remain proud of the Cusack family legacy and enjoy welcoming visitors to coffee and conversation after the 8:15 a.m. Sunday Mass.

Holy Trinity,
– Colorado Springs –

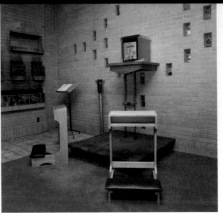

*O*n August 28, 1959, Archbishop Urban J. Vehr of the Denver Archdiocese established the parish of Holy Trinity in Colorado Springs. Land was acquired from A.V. (Tony) Venetucci, who owned land in the Venetian Village neighborhood.

Father John L. Aylward the founding pastor arrived at Holy Trinity who at the time had 450 families, but no buildings. Mass was held in the Crazy Cat Lounge, a bar on North Nevada . With a few linens and a traveling Mass kit, Father said Mass. The parish eventually found more suitable surroundings: a Laundromat at 3003 N. Institute, before washers and dryers were installed. Father Aylward died in 1963, and Father Walter Jaeger became the second pastor of Holy Trinity. He found that this new parish was already planning to build a school. Father Jaeger broke ground with a golden shovel in January 1965. A year later, the school opened. Father Jaeger was pastor until 1971. Next, Father Edward T. Madden strengthened the parish's missionary role. Father Michael A. Walsh became Holy Trinity's fourth pastor on September 6, 1976. In January of 1977, the parish council recommended that a new church be built for the rapidly growing parish. In 1978, Father Walsh and Bishop Richard Hanifen broke ground for the new building. The last pew was set in place in June 1979, two months before the 20th anniversary.

Holy Trinity finished the "complete and modern parish" which Father Aylward had dreamed of in 1959. In June 1982, Father George V. Fagan was named pastor until 1985. In 1985, Father Karl Useldinger was named pastor; he was succeeded by Father John Auer in 1989. From 1996-2004, Ms. CoCo Soper was assigned as Parish Director. During her tenure, diocesan and Holy Cross priests celebrated the Sacraments at Holy Trinity. Father Mark Zacker was assigned as Pastor from 2004-2008. Holy Trinity School celebrated its 40th anniversary, and closing, during the 2006-2007 academic year. Declining enrollment and increased costs led to the permanent closure of the school in May of 2007. Father Jim Williams, a native son of Holy Trinity Parish, began serving as full time Pastor in February 2008.

As Holy Trinity Parish looks forward to celebrating it's 50th anniversary in 2009. Cesar Chavez Academy (Charter School) will be leasing the school building at the start of the 2008 school year. Improvements are ongoing to the parish's facilities. The parish also continues to build and support its various ministries according to the Diocesan Pastoral Plan, in the areas of faith formation, evangelization, leadership, social justice, and stewardship.

*T*he Immaculate Conception community traces its origins back to 1993, when a small group of individuals wrote to Bishop Richard Hanifen asking for permission to use the Latin Mass from the 1962 Missal, in conformance with the permission provided by Pope John Paul II in the 1984 indult, *"Quattuor abhinc Anno,"* and the 1988 motu proprio, *"Ecclesia Dei."*

Bishop Hanifen organized an oversight committee with diocesan leaders and the leadership team of the Latin Mass Community to address issues, including the organization of the new community, logistics and effective integration into the diocesan fold — in conformance with all diocesan guidelines, requirements, and business practices.

The Latin Mass Community held its inaugural Mass in 1994 at St. Mary's Cathedral, where it remained until a renovation project prompted a move to St. Joseph in Fountain in 2002. At first, one Mass was celebrated monthly; this grew to two, and finally to a full weekly schedule, plus holy days.

The thriving community gained permission to use its current name, Immaculate Conception of the Blessed Mother of God. Significant growth, including families with small children, precipitated religious education programs. Conversations with the Priestly Fraternity of St. Peter, beginning in 2001, resulted in the appointment of Father Thomas Fristchen as chaplain the next year. A stable member of the diocese with a special mission to engage Catholics preferring the Latin Mass, the community reaches out to them, providing a safe and friendly environment.

Bishops Hanifen and Michael J. Sheridan have played essential roles in the community's founding. Father Don Dunn, the cathedral's recently retired rector, provided generous support and guidance, and two chaplains, Father Rawley Myers, who served from 1994 until 2002, and Father Fritschen, who arrived in 2002, have fostered growth, including the 2006 purchase of a church facility in Security.

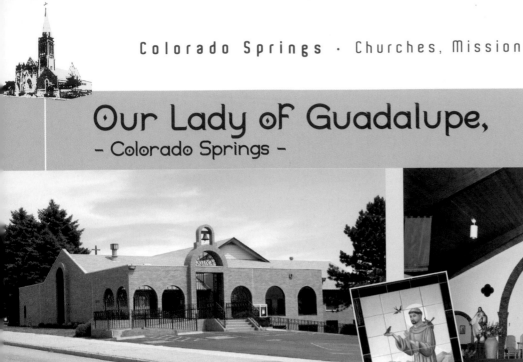

Our Lady of Guadalupe,
– Colorado Springs –

*F*or more than a half a century, Our Lady of Guadalupe has served a diverse community of Catholics in Colorado Springs, becoming a home away from home for many. For more than a decade, parishioners have collaborated with Catholic Charities, supporting a strong English as a Second Language program and helping Spanish-speaking Latinos acquire important language skills. Parishioners also serve the local Church in its mission of advocacy for the area's growing and diverse Latino population, embracing the faith and cultural traditions of Latino Catholics.

The parish strives to be a refuge of faith, hope and love to a mosaic-style community, welcoming all to learn and celebrate. Parishioners participate in a number of multicultural and multilingual missions, fostering spiritual growth and religious education, offering health and community information, and organizing an array of youth activities. The parish produces a monthly newsletter for youngsters, chronicling service projects and fundraisers, including one to raise more than $300 toward a summer project, "Acquire the Fire."

Parishioners' drive to serve the community and each other originates in their long-standing commitment to what Jesus Christ asks of his followers: "I was hungry and you gave me food, I was thirsty and you gave me drink, a stranger and you welcomed me, naked, and you clothed me, ill and you care for me, in prison and you visit me" (Mt 25: 35, 36).

The parish is proud of its Catholic identity, its cultural diversity and its heritage and embraces Our Lady of Guadalupe not just as its patroness, but also as its Spiritual Mother and the star for its new evangelization efforts.

Our Lady of Perpetual Help,
- Manitou Springs -

*T*he history of Catholicism in the Pikes Peak region can be traced back to 1860, when Father Joseph Machebeuf celebrated the first Mass in Old Colorado City. Later, as the first bishop of Denver, he established the area's first Catholic church, Our Lady of Perpetual Help, in Manitou in 1882. The structure was sold in 1886 for use as a residence. A second church was constructed in 1889; Bishop John Joseph Hennessey celebrated the first Mass in the new church in July. A suspicious fire completely destroyed this church on the night of August 3, 1903.

Father Andreas Casey immediately began rebuilding. Contributions from a benefactor, General Palmer, and anonymous donors and Father Casey's personal salary completely covered the construction costs. Completed in three months, the 1903 church continues to serve the Manitou Springs Catholic faith community.

In 1893 Father Jean Baptiste Francolon, who had just become pastor, built the "castle" — today Miramont — as the rectory, where he and his mother lived until 1900.

Father M.P. Callanan, who was pastor in 1905, built a replica of the Lourdes Grotto in memory of his mother. When the Oblates of Mary Immaculate assumed pastoral leadership of Sacred Heart in Colorado Springs in 1926, Our Lady of Perpetual Help was included in their territory. The Congregation of Holy Cross replaced the Oblates in 1984 and continued the relationship among Our Lady of Perpetual Help, Holy Rosary in Cascade and Sacred Heart.

The rectory has served as a meeting place for parish groups. Named Schultz House in honor of Father James Schultz, C.S.C., a staff member at Holy Cross Novitiate killed in a mountain-climbing accident, the rectory serves as a gathering place after Sunday Mass.

Today Our Lady of Perpetual Help is a small, young and vibrant community, part of the Sacred Heart Tri-Community. Its lively Sunday liturgies welcome everyone.

Our Lady of the Pines,
– Colorado Springs –

a group of Catholics gathered in 1960 to discuss the need for a church in Black Forest. Religious instruction for children, their first priority, was offered in private homes, then at the caretaker's home on Brentwood Estates, followed by a move to a log cabin behind the Black Forest Store. The first Mass was celebrated in 1962 with more than 250 people in attendance. A chaplain from the Air Force Academy offered a field Mass in 1963, and Father Wood, a chaplain at St. Francis Hospital, celebrated Mass weekly in 1964 at the "Sugar Shack." That same year, Denver's Archbishop Vehr approved a $50,000 donation for a church, and during its construction phase, the faith community worshiped at a log church belonging to The Black Forest Community Church.

The first Mass at Our Lady of the Pines Catholic Church was celebrated in 1965. Mission priests served the parish 1965 to 1967. Father Thomas Hanlon became the first resident priest in 1970, and a rectory was built during his stay. The growing parish added an annex to the church in 1987, doubling seating capacity and adding six classrooms and a kitchen.

With nearly 600 families in the early 1990s, parishioners formed a Knights of Columbus Council and several social ministry programs. Within a decade, crowds stood on the porches, trying to "hear" Mass. A larger church constructed in 2004 added a 24-hour Blessed Sacrament Chapel. The parish now includes nearly 900 families. Parishioners plan to construct a new parish life center to house a parish hall, classrooms, and offices to meet the needs of the ever-growing ministries. The parish truly lives its mission derived from Scripture: "Your light must shine before others, that they may see your good deeds and glorify your heavenly Father" (Mt 5:16).

*T*he first meeting to discuss the creation of a mission church in Elbert County took place in 1995. The area's first Mass was offered at St. Mark Fellowship Hall in Kiowa in April 1996, and a month later services were held off County Road 17 in "The Upper Room," which became the mission's temporary worship space between 1996 and 1997. Parishioners formed a youth ministry and established the first vacation Bible school at Casey Jones Park in 1997, the same year they purchased land for a new church. Design preparations underway, the mission's 183 families gathered under a tent for an outdoor Mass in summer 1997 on its property. Father Brian Q. Mohan was installed as the first Pastor in august 2007.

Bishop Richard Hanifen broke ground for the new church in spring 1998, and at the end of November celebrated the dedication Mass. The Knights of Columbus sponsored its first Epiphany party in January 1998, the same year the parish held its first R.C.I.A class. Father Jim Williams was appointed as the first pastoral administrator in 1999 and lived in the new rectory. The first ministry fair was held in 1999.

A stained-glass window was installed in 2000, the same year parishioners welcomed Father Khanh K. Pham Nguyen as the second pastoral administrator. Father Dennis Dwyer, who had celebrated the area's first Mass in 1996, returned in March 2001 as the third pastoral administrator, and the parish's first group received First Holy Communion in May that year.

A Saturday evening Mass was added to the schedule in October 2002, and Bishop Michael Sheridan visited for the first time in 2003. Parishioners dedicated the Queen of Heaven Cemetery in 2004. Bishop Sheridan conducted Confirmation services in 2005, and the parish marked its 10th anniversary with a celebration on May 31, 2006.

Our Lady of Victory,
- Limon -

𝓂any years prior to the official dedication of Our Lady of Victory, Catholics in Limon celebrated Mass twice a month in the basement of the old Bank Hotel and later in a theater. (A tornado destroyed the Bank Hotel in June 1990.) Priests traveled to the area by train or "jitney," carrying a Mass kit with the necessary articles for services. Led by Henry Thibault, parishioners constructed the first church over a two-year period, and Bishop Henry Tihen dedicated it in 1925. Our Lady of Victory shared a pastor with a parish in Hugo. This original church is the present site of St. Mary in Flagler. Parishioners purchased a converted Army barracks in 1947 and adapted it as parish hall.

Priests from Denver served from 1925 until the Diocese of Colorado Springs was established in 1984. Father Jerry Kelleher served from 1984 to 1992, when Father Bill Rhinehard, a Vincentian, became pastor. The Vincentian Fathers committed themselves to the diocese's eastern plains for a decade.

The present church was constructed and dedicated in 1961. Parishioners built a new rectory in 1994 to accommodate the move of the resident priest from Hugo to Limon. St. Anthony in Hugo and St. Mary in Flagler are now missions of the parish.

*E*stablished in 1987 on the concept of lay leadership with Jeff Kelling as mission organizer and parish director, Pax Christi serves the diocese's northern area. Forty families gathered for the first Mass in the Northridge Elementary School gymnasium in 1988. Jesuits from Sacred Heart Retreat House and Regis University and other priests served the mission, which moved to its present location at the end of 1998. Dedicated in 1999, the chapel and multi-use building fostered fellowship. Father Kenneth Przybyla became the first pastor in 2000, the same year parishioners constructed a new worship space.

Dedicated that same year, the circular worship space features the Table of the Word (ambo), the Table of the Eucharist (altar), and a chair from which the priest may preside over the assembly. A prominent font and immersion pool are used in baptismal celebrations. The multi-use building was retrofitted into a bi-level social, educational and office facility. Parishioners created a labyrinth in 2006 for prayer and reflection.

The religious education programs serve more than 1,000 pre-school through 12th graders. Volunteers also reach out to the larger community in many ways. They hold semi-annual blood drives, supply bread and food to the homeless in Denver and provide Christmas gifts for the community's needy. Parishioners glean crops through the COMPA ministry, mentor the imprisoned and serve lunches monthly at the Samaritan House, a Denver homeless shelter. They support Southern Exposure, which builds homes in Juarez, Mexico. To raise awareness of the Fair Trade movement, fair trade coffee is sold after weekend Masses. The parish invites Third World Market and non-profit organizations to use facilities to sell goods that provide living-wage income for their constituents. Offertory collections are tithed to support local agencies. These activities foster spiritual growth in meaningful and life-changing ways.

Sacred Heart,
– Cheyenne Wells –

*F*athers G. Raber, Felix Abel, and John Krenske served the Catholics in Cheyenne Wells from 1909 to 1912 when the bishop of Denver purchased property for $1. Construction of a church began in 1913 and was completed by October. Reverend Matthew, CSSR, from Denver celebrated the first Mass in the new mission that year. Father Aloysius Kiefer, called "the Padre of the Plains," became the first permanent pastor in 1918. A 10-room bungalow constructed at that time as a rectory remains in use for that purpose today. Sacred Heart School was built in 1921, but the 1920s crash of the cattle market caused the parish to fall into debt. Father Kieffer began his famous Living Rosary Crusade to raise funds. Funds collected after the crash were donated to foreign missions, but he also constructed the parish hall for social and recreational purposes in 1949. After more than 40 years of service as a priest, Father Kieffer discontinued his ministry in 1952 because of failing eyesight.

The Bethlehem Fathers — Father Francis Brem and his assistant Father Peter Wildhaber — served the parish for three years until 1955, when Father John Cajar was named pastor. By this time, the congregation had outgrown the church, and the parish hall was converted to the worship space, dedicated in 1957. Found to be unsafe, the original church was demolished in 1958. The parish closed the school in 1971, after more than 58 years of service. The last graduation of eighth graders occurred in 1970. With funds from a good wheat crop and a generous legacy from Father Kieffer, who died in 1971, the church was remodeled that year.

Among Sacred Heart's outreach activities is a food pantry, established in the 1990s, that serves the entire community. St. Augustine in Kit Carson is a mission of this parish.

Sacred Heart, today's standard bearer of the Tri-Community, itself was once the mission church of Our Lady of Perpetual Help in Manitou Springs. Organized in the 1880s at 26th Street and Robinson Avenue, it was known as St. Mary's Church of Old Colorado City, where it served about thirty families.

The present mission-style church was constructed in 1921, dedicated along with the rectory by Bishop J. Henry Tihen of Denver in 1922. Father H.V. Darley spearheaded the construction, and the parish was renamed Sacred Heart.

The Oblates of Mary Immaculate assumed pastoral responsibility for both Sacred Heart and Our Lady of Perpetual Help in 1926 and served the parish for nearly 60 years. The Sisters of Notre Dame de Namur arrived in 1928, purchased land for a convent and rest home and taught Sunday school. The Sisters encouraged the building of a school, which finally came to fruition in 1954 with grades one through four located in two houses until a school building was completed and dedicated in 1955. The Benedictine Sisters of Atchison, Kan., oversaw the school, which closed in 1981.

When the Diocese of Colorado Springs was formed in 1984, the

Oblates withdrew from Sacred Heart. The Congregation of Holy Cross from Notre Dame, Ind., then assumed pastoral care of the parish and of churches in Manitou Springs and Cascade.

The church sanctuary was remodeled in 1992 to serve the community better. To honor Father LeRoy Clementich, C.S.C., the Hispanic community presented the parish with a shrine of Our Lady of Guadalupe. The parish began to work more closely with the parishes in Manitou Springs and Cascade in 1996, referring to themselves as the Tri-Community — "three communities, one parish."

Saint Andrew Kim,
– Colorado Springs –

𝓛ed by Sister Immaclatha Park in 1977, the Korean Catholic community originated with seven Colorado Springs families, who met thrice monthly. Father Hector, a member of the Guadalupe mission, celebrated the first Korean-language Mass at St. Francis Hospital Chapel. Korean Catholics numbered 20 families by 1981, including many military families from Fort Carson. They attended Mass at Holy Trinity, and Sister Teresa Han taught catechism. Father Peter Ryu, (Chang-sun) a Korean Jesuit living in Denver, celebrated Mass in Korean monthly. Community members attended Mass in English at St. Joseph in 1982, but Father Benedict Suh (Suk-Tae), a priest at the Denver Korean Catholic Community Church, celebrated weekly Mass in Korean in 1983 in Colorado Springs.

Between 1985 and 1987, several Korean priests served Denver's and Colorado Springs' Korean Catholics, but in 1987, Father Philips Kim (Cha-Gyu) became the first permanent pastor of both communities, followed by Father Peter Huh in 1988. Sister Leticia Choi helped Father Huh full time. Parishioners organized the first Legion of Mary chapter in 1989, and began a special collection for the construction of a church, which started in 1996. Although parishioners donated building funds, they also raised money by collecting soda cans and bottles, making and selling foods such as mandoo, chili peppers, bul-go-gi and jab-che, and through

garage sales. Completed in 1997, the church was named St. Andrew Kim. Father Berchman Lee (Yong-Woo) was the parish priest.

Parishioners donate to causes worldwide, invite speakers from a variety of countries and send priests to conferences around the world. Volunteers attend and help organize retreats and rallies locally and in Mexico. The area's sole Korean-American community, the congregation reaches out to other Koreans and to the area's needy, working hard to serve the larger community.

Saint Anthony Padua,
- Hugo -

*H*ugo was once known as Willow Springs, a stage stop along the trail to Denver between 1859 and 1870, when the Kansas Pacific Railroad was extended to Denver. Hugo Catholics were served by traveling priests. The tiny Catholic community built a small church — 20 feet wide and 30 feet long — in 1901 and dedicated it to St. Anthony of Padua. The Franciscan Fathers took care of the Hugo mission and others along the Kansas Pacific and Rock Island railroad lines. Father Michael Horgan was appointed pastor in 1923. When a rectory was constructed in 1924, parishioners moved the church to a site next door. They added a sacristy, and a wall dividing the living space from the sanctuary was removed to accommodate the increasing congregation. Father Horgan also served the missions of Limon, Deer Trail and Strasburg.

Father Horgan taught religious education classes until 1928, when the Sisters of Charity came to teach vacation summer school and continued annually until 1949. Parishioners formed an Altar and Rosary Society and the Gentleman's Club, two parish committees.

Tragedy struck in 1945 when Father Horgan was injured in a car crash and died, after having served as pastor for 22 years. Father John W. Scannell, appointed pastor in 1945, introduced the envelope tithing system.

Parishioners dedicated a new church in 1950 in the same spot as the original one. The Hugo Catholic Calvary Cemetery was founded in 1950. Parishioners established the annual parish bazaar and dinner and began staffing a refreshment booth at the Lincoln County Fair. In the mid-1950s, street preaching began with a Vincentian priest from Denver's St. Thomas Seminary and two deacons, who spent two weeks each summer answering questions about Catholicism in the park area off Main Street.

Parishioners continue to serve the community through an array of outreach ministries.

Saint Augustine,
– Kit Carson –

𝒮t. Augustine began in the 1880s, when a Franciscan priest visited Kit Carson. Mass was celebrated in the early 1900s in the schoolhouse. Fund-raising events paid for a church that was eventually completed in 1920. In 1916, Willia Rhoades donated land for a church in Kit Carson. In May 1918, construction for the church began. The exact date of the first official Mass in the newly constructed church has been lost to history, but it was either late 1919 or early 1920.

Father Alphonse Keiffer served as pastor of St. Augustine from 1909 to 1953. In 1950, Father Francis Brem came to assist at the parish. After Father Keiffer retired, Father Brem became pastor. Father John Canjar served as the pastor from 1955 to 1959. In 1959 Father George Kearney became pastor and led the dedication ceremony for the current church in May 1965.

From 1966 to 1984, St. Augustine had six different pastors. In 1984, St. Augustine became part of the Diocese of Colorado Springs and Father James Halloran was assigned its pastor. From 1988 to 2002, St. Augustine had five different pastors; in 2004 Father Jaimes Ponce became parish administrator.

*I*n the late 1800s Falcon thrived with a hotel, a bank, two blacksmith shops and a few saloons. By the turn of the century, the railroad tracks that had been the town's lifeline became unnecessary and the town all but disappeared.

At the turn of the millennium, however, Falcon has again become the center of the county's population expansion and economic development. By 2004 a handful of Catholic families began discussing the need for a parish church and school. They brought the idea to Bishop Michael Sheridan, already aware of the area's population projection, who called a community meeting with diocesan officials in 2005 in Falcon Middle School gymnasium. The bishop guessed that, by word of mouth, 20 or 25 interested Catholics might come.

Instead, 120 attended; on Ash Wednesday of the same year, a special Mass offered in the gym attracted 200 faithful. Falcon's Catholic Community began celebrating Mass every Sunday that May, led by Father Paul Wicker, pastor of Holy Apostles. Father Paul proved a vital force in promoting this new faith community, serving as its canonical pastor.

Bishop Sheridan designated the faith community a quasi-parish on July 22, 2005, the feast of St. Benedict, naming it for the saint and honoring the newly elected Pope Benedict XVI.

Currently, the diocese's newest parish serves more than 200 families who have formed a full array of outreach ministries.

Saint Catherine of Siena,
- Burlington -

a priest would come to the eastern plains from Colorado Springs monthly in 1910 to celebrate Mass in private homes. Worshipers used chairs, wooden benches and occasionally bales of hay as seating. The community of St. Catherine of Siena attained parish status in 1916, the year a small wood-frame church was built. Priests from St. Charles Borromeo in Stratton served the church until Father Joseph Lane became the first resident pastor in 1949.

The parish established a building fund in 1969 for a new church. Groundbreaking took place in 1975, and Archbishop James Casey dedicated it in 1979. Parishioners retired the mortgage in December 1986. During this time, religious education classes were held in the Knights of Columbus hall and at a nearby Lutheran church. Youth programs quickly outgrew their facilities, and parishioners and the pastor created a fundraising drive for a parish hall. Groundbreaking for the new facility took place in 1996, and the mortgage was paid in full a

decade later. In addition to the youth ministry, parishioners organized an array of outreach efforts, including a prison ministry and a Hispanic committee, among others.

Vandals desecrated the church and set it afire in 2004. Father Francisco Quezada, pastor, called for diocesan parishes — particularly those on the plains — and for churches around the nation to help and to lend financial support to the restoration. The church was reconstructed by parishioners who provided the wood furnishings, the great cross, door handles, the bronze statue of Our Lady of Guadalupe, the bell tower and the louvers. The statue of St. Catherine of Siena — the only one to have survived the fire unscathed — the rebuilt Stations of the Cross and the original processional cross from the destroyed church remain in the reconstructed one as constant reminders of the parish's struggles. Bishop Michael Sheridan dedicated the new church in 2005.

Saint Charles Borromeo,
– Stratton –

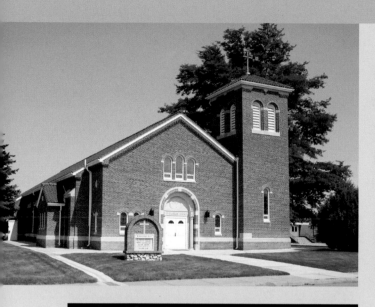

*A*fter celebrating Mass once a month in a hall above a bank, Stratton Catholics constructed St. Charles Borromeo Church in 1910. Father Alphonse Keiffer was appointed the first pastor in 1913, and parishioners built a two-story rectory in 1915, followed by an academy in 1920. The Great Depression and drought brought hardship, but timely rains returned, bringing good crops. Donations of time and treasure made possible a new, larger church, dedicated in 1949. A large hall, auditorium, kitchen and dining facilities were constructed and dedicated in 1952.

The parish closed the academy in 1969 and razed the building, leaving a vacant lot. In an effort to eliminate the taxes on the church's unimproved lot, Father Will Menard created prayer parks, called "Our Lady of the Plains" and "Our Lord of the Plains." Garage and bake sales, memorial donations, volunteerism and financial contributions funded the gardens. Adorned with bronze statues created by Herberto Maestas of San Luis and

Norbert Ohnmacht of Burlington, these parks draw travelers from I-70, tour groups and other visitors.

The parish emphasizes vocations to the priesthood. Three young parishioners have entered the priesthood; one is studying to be a permanent deacon and eight women have entered religious life. Religious education classes continue for children and adults.

Parishioners established the annual St. Charles Bazaar, originally as the Fall Festival and the Harvest Festival. The event began as a way to erase parish debt, but it has grown into a tradition. The Altar Rosary Society serves dinner, and parishioners run bingo and carnival games, a quilt raffle, and a reverse raffle, making the bazaar a popular community event as well as a fundraiser.

When St. Catherine of Siena Church in Burlington was destroyed by fire in 2004, St. Charles provided spiritual support and facilities.

Saint Francis of Assisi,
– Castle Rock –

*T*he history of St. Francis of Assisi parish in Castle Rock begins in the Gold Rush days of 1865. Mass was offered for the miners in the Lake Gulch schoolhouse and in private homes. With a gift from the William Dixon family, the stone church in the city square was begun and finally dedicated on Dec. 16, 1888.

In 1911, St. Francis became a mission of Colorado Springs and for years, until 1930, Franciscan friars from Denver served the community as one of six churches in the entire area. Until 1930 no priest was assigned for regular services, but the Franciscans continued to offer Mass and the sacraments until early 1950, when Father Walter Steidel from Denver was appointed pastor. He traveled 75 miles each Sunday to say Mass in St. Francis as well as in the six other churches.

By 1960, the stone church had become inadequate for the needs of the growing Catholic population in the area. The present site of St. Francis, on hill with an un-obstructed view of Pike's Peak, was chosen in 1965, and a new wooden church was built and dedicated in 1966. The stone church was then turned into a restaurant which still operates in the town square.

The parish of St. Francis is once again forced into expansion mode with the number of Catholics moving into the Douglas County area. This county has consistently been listed as one of the fastest-growing counties in the entire nation, and the increase in the number of

Catholics is reflected in that growth. Faith and dedication will shape the vision of the future of St. Francis of Assisi Parish.

When visitors enter the grounds of Mt. St. Francis, they realize that they are in a special place, peaceful and beautiful. The area, home to the Province of St. Joseph of the Sisters of St. Francis of Perpetual Adoration, is also the location of St. Francis of Assisi Parish. After a band of local families started to attend Mass in the Sisters' chapel, built in 1963, Bishop Richard Hanifen gave mission status to what is now called St. Francis of Assisi Parish. It was made a parish in 1987. In 1989 the Diocese of Colorado Springs and the Sisters signed a 50-year agreement that allows St. Francis of Assisi Parish to remain in this special place with the Sisters.

St. Francis continued to grow and, with permission of the Sisters, renovated the chapel to accommodate more people. The parish built an addition to provide for meeting/classrooms and a parish hall. The community continues to use and enjoy the facilities.

Having been blessed by God and by association with the Sisters, the community goes forth from the mountain to all parts of the Colorado Springs community and to the world. The parish has believed and acts upon the call of the Spirit to love as Jesus loves by supporting the diocese and the local community through various activities. For example, once a month the church family serves at the Marian House, the Catholic Charities soup kitchen. In partnership with Sunrise United Methodist, a Habitat for Humanity house has been built. Many other service-oriented activities are part of the core of St. Francis of Assisi Parish.

St. Francis of Assisi continues to strive to be a Eucharistic community, blessed by God, called by the Spirit, and sent to love as Jesus loves.

Saint Gabriel the Archangel,
– Colorado Springs –

*S*aint Gabriel began as Metro North Mission in 1998, with the guiding vision of the Metro North Regional Pastoral Council, the pastors, parish director, and Father Paul Wicker, the regional Episcopal Vicar. More than two hundred people gathered for the first Mass, celebrated at Mountain Ridge Middle School with Father Wicker as presider. Soon after, Father Gus Stewart was assigned as administrator, and with this appointment, the church status was elevated from mission to quasi-parish before attaining parish status in 2000 with Father Stewart named as first pastor. In July 2008, Father C. Robert Manning was named second pastor.

efforts to and support of the growing Hispanic community under the guidance of Father Gene Emrisek and Father Frank Quezada serving as sacramental ministers.

The parish of Saint Gabriel the Archangel in Colorado Springs is young in more ways than one. Not only is the parish one of the newest in the diocese, but many parishioners are young families who are recent transplants to Colorado Springs. A major percentage of parishioners' families have links to the armed forces, and the transient nature of their lifestyle influences their high-energy participation in the parish.

The parish welcomes new members in myriad ways, including offering many roles for volunteers to help serve and guide the parish and the wider community. Worshipers are greeted warmly before each celebration, and newcomers are formally introduced to the parish at welcome dinners that are held several times a year. Volunteers serve the parish in catechetical, liturgical, and fellowship roles.

Parishioners began a three-year capital campaign in 2001 and formed a committee to start the architectural design process for a church building. Ground-breaking took place in 2003, and the first construction phase was completed in 2004. The parish's first Spanish Mass was celebrated in 2005, the culmination of its outreach

As the parish, its buildings, and its families continue to grow, so does the joyful spirit of their worship and service to others.

*R*esidents of the Southgate neighborhood in southwest Colorado Springs petitioned Bishop Urban J. Vehr for a new church in their area in 1966, and in that same year, the bishop appointed Father Dean Kumba as the founding pastor of St. Joseph. Groundbreaking for a church took place in 1967. The new church was dedicated in 1968 on the feast of St. Joseph the Worker with more than 500, including 100 priests, in attendance. The new facility included a worship space for more than 400, two classrooms, a new social hall, and parish offices. Giaccomo V. Mussner of Bolzano, Italy, sculpted the statuary and the Stations of the Cross.

The parish thrived, reaching 700 families in 1995 and then 1000 families by 1999. The parish submitted a study and petition to the bishop for an expanded long-term facility in 1995, and this plan was approved in 2000. Parishioners pledged more than $1 million for a $1.5 million project, and groundbreaking occurred on Christmas Day 2000. The nave of the church was enhanced by a baptismal font; an additional two wings increased seating by 165 people. Six classrooms were built, and a nursery was added. A large social hall that seats up to 300 people and includes a large commercial kitchen were also built.

St. Joseph began as and remains a parish that serves the area's working people. Parishioners represent many ethnic and cultural backgrounds and are committed to developing and implementing programs that foster spiritual growth and create and support a car-

ing spiritual network for the community. They empower strong leaders and volunteers to design outreach opportunities serving the area's poor and marginalized. Liturgical volunteers strive to make worship relevant, heartfelt and memorable.

St. Joseph has marked its 40th anniversary as a parish in 2008, a milestone observed with celebrative activities throughout the year.

Saint Joseph,
- Fountain -

When the Denver Rio Grande Railroad was built between 1871 and 1872, Fountain consisted of four to six recognizable blocks and 100 residents of whom a dozen were Catholics. They celebrated Mass in private homes and later at the Mission of Corpus Christi and the Mission of Pauline Chapel. The Catholic Extension Society purchased the Heidelburg Inn in 1936 for use as a church. Built in 1918 as the First National Bank of Fountain, then defunct in the Crash of 1929, it had been converted into the inn, a beer parlor. After the purchase of the bank-turned-inn, Sisters came from St. Mary in Colorado Springs to teach religious education classes. Weekly confessions were observed, and Mass celebrated. The First Methodist Church of Colorado donated pews to the fledgling community.

Sisters of Loretto and Sisters of Victory Noll taught religious education classes in 1950. In the early 1960s, parishioners formed the Catholic Women's Association, and the Legion of Mary. They donated new vestments, and, in 1969, a new organ. A beautiful Mariachi Mass was sung in the garden on the church's north side in

June 1969. Ground was broken in 1980 for the basement of a new church in the form of a Fort Carson chapel which was moved from the army post to church property. The new church was dedicated in 1982.

A welcoming community, the parish continues its religious education classes and Bible study. The parish supports Fountain Valley Ministries, which works with local government agencies to assist the needy with emergency funds for rent, utilities, prescriptions and other needs. Share Colorado uses parish facilities as a distribution site as does Alcoholics Anonymous, which holds weekly meetings. The parish serves its small community through sacraments and outreach activities. Recently discussion has begun to join the parish to Holy Family under the new name of St. Dominic.

*F*ather Henry Robinson celebrated Salida's first Mass in 1875 in the home of the Burnett family. Father P.J. Gleason became Salida's first resident pastor in 1885, celebrating Mass at Central School because fire had destroyed a small frame church that Father Robinson is said to have built in1880. A new church, constructed in 1889, served about 55 Catholic families living in Salida and in Buena Vista; this structure later became a school. The present church — built in 1909 — was listed as one of the most beautiful churches in the state for its plaster ceiling, painted with six circular symbols. Parishioners donated the statuary and the Stations of the Cross. The parish built a new school in 1957.

Water leakage prompted parishioners to brick the sanctuary window and carpet the floor. After the plaster ceiling cracked and fell in the 1970s, wood paneling was installed to prevent injuries. Later, a room added to the church provided space for the sacristy and a restroom. In the 1990s, a large canopy was removed from the sanctuary and the pastor, Father Joseph Halloran, hung a large icon of Jesus in its place, flanked by two icons of archangels.

The school was closed in 1990. Two years later, the public school system used the building for its students until 1999. The Knights of Columbus use it on weekends for bingo, and religious education classes for students from kindergarten through high school take place there. Texas Tech University geological students use the building in summer.

A church renovation began in 1995; the rear sacristy became a reconciliation chapel, and sheet rock replaced the paneled ceiling. The sanctuary's paneled back wall was removed, and the bricked-up window was opened and filled with stained glass. The church was rededicated in 1997.

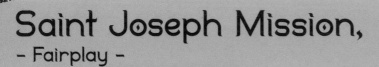
Saint Joseph Mission,
– Fairplay –

a mission of St. Rose of Lima, St. Joseph was established in 1874 as part of the Diocese of Denver. Now part of the Diocese of Colorado Springs, the mission serves about 80 families, many full-time and some part-time residents who may live in larger metropolitan settings but who spend winters in the area's warmer climate.

The mission formed a number of councils staffed by volunteers. The Altar Council remains after Sunday services to clean and prepare the church for the coming week. Members of the Hospitality Committee greet all who enter the church and arrange for weekly snacks for the fellowship that follows every Sunday Mass. They also provide get-well cards for those who are ill and for other special occasions. The Music Committee selects the sacred liturgical music and participates in the choirs.

The Sacristan Committee maintains supplies for each liturgy, attends to the collection baskets and contributions to maintenance and building security while the Worship and Spiritual Growth Committee focuses on training and scheduling Eucharistic ministers, lectors and readers, and providing sacramental preparation materials for catechists and other spiritual development programs. The Social Ministry donates to local stores, social service agencies and lodging houses for the needy. A weekly Bible study group fosters spiritual growth, and a dinner club hosts monthly gatherings to promote fellowship.

Two appointed members serve on the Finance Council and assist the pastor as advisors with respect to the disbursement, use, and distribution of parish funds.

The mission shares an office and a mailing address with St. Rose of Lima.

*P*lans for a parish in fast-growing Douglas County in the nothern end of our diocese have been a long time in the making. Although discussions had been in process as to a location of a parish in the western Highland Ranch area it was not until a tract of land and a priest became available that a formal faith community was possible. At two meetings hosted by St. Thomas More (Centennial) and St. Mary (Littleton), more than 150 families expressed serious interest in a new church in that area. They gathered for dinners at Padre Restaurant and formed liturgical and educational ministries, and Bishop Richard Hanifen granted them the patron St. Mark. With St. Mark officially established in 2002, more than 1,200 worshipers gathered for three inaugural Masses on Easter Sunday.

Bishop Hanifen had already dedicated the property in 2001, and parishioners began site and financial planning for a church, choosing an architect and a contractor. Parishioners held meetings throughout 2001-2002 to discuss needs and desires for the land and to form development, finance and design councils. Many people, including the pastoral staff, contributed countless hours to shepherd the process through to the groundbreaking, held in March 2004. St. Mark was dedicated on the feast of St. Mark, April 25, 2005.

Over 900 families formed more than 50 ministries. A social justice ministry addresses injustice locally, nationally and globally through direct service and activities that foster social change. Volunteers glean local farmers'

fields, donating the second harvest — that would have been tilled back into the soil — to Colorado's hungry. Youth groups with adult leaders visit La Puente Home serving the homeless, providing hygiene kits to migrant workers there. The Knights of Columbus, Mothers of St. Mark, the men's group and the Thread Bearers, among others, nurture fellowship and service.

Saint Mary,
- Flagler -

*E*stablished in 1947, St. Mary was established in Flagler, one of Colorado's smallest towns, when Father Henry Ernst was pastor of St. Charles in Stratton and Mass was celebrated in the home of Vernon Nau. The mission's first church, located on 8th Street, included pews from Brighton, courtesy of George Hubbard and Charles Keller, who transported them to St. Mary in 1947. The Stations of the Cross — a gift from Vernon Nau's uncle — were added in 1948, the same year six families raised $2,300 to buy four lots and a 30-by-22-foot school building, which was moved from Idalia, Colorado.

A new larger church was carefully moved along Highway 24 from Limon in 1959 and doubled the seating capacity. The footing and foundation for the new structure were built by church members, and the steeple and cross had been removed for the move to 4th Street.

Currently, St. Mary is a mission of Our Lady of Victory in Limon.

$\mathcal{E}$stablished in 1990, St. Mary of the Rockies serves the eastern section of Park County along Highway 285, west of the Kenosha Pass. Bailey is not a true town, but has a post office that serves more than 3,850 far flung mail boxes in the area, plus Pine, Shawnee and Grant boxes. Many residents are in subdivisions that are considered "neighborhoods" of the parish.

With the parishioners doing the construction, a new church and parish center was completed in 2001. A scenic cross tower with tuned chimes greets those who arrive and leave the church, and a large decorative steel sign built on an attractive formation of large rocks calls attention to its location, both of which were designed and crafted by long time parishioner, Bernard Karnowka. Bernard also crafted in the church the baptismal font, metal candle stands for the altar, the votive light stand, and the original small tabernacle which was used before the new church was built.

Current Pastor, Father Patrick W. Battiato, refers to the hillside upon which the church and rectory lay as "Mary's Hill," with the strong belief that the parish patron, Mary Queen of Heaven, plays a crucial role in protecting and guiding the parish community. Evangelization has been a strong effort, reaching out particularly to Catholics in the area who do not attend Mass or participate in the community. Many letters are sent to both "active" and "inactive" lists of parishioners. Several ads have been published in local newspapers calling all area Catholics "home!" In addition, a strong effort is being made to increase the parish finances, both through increased offertory appeals and various fund raisers. Weekly Fish Fry's during Lent, and the monthly dinners throughout the year do much to gather the parish community together, creating an increased experience of fellowship and unity. Father puts a strong emphasis on the reality that all of God's people are called, by their Baptism, to live as God's priestly people, "being the presence of Christ" in the midst of the world. Focusing on the necessity of living life "from the inside out," personal prayer, religious education at every level, traditional devotions throughout the week, including the rosary before every Mass, and all day Eucharistic Adoration each Thursday have been added. Beautiful liturgical music and an attractive church environment do much to enhance a mystical experience. Societies dedicated to St. Joseph the Worker and St. Therese of Lisieux seek to deepen the spiritual lives of the people. With a small number of children and young adults, special events are offered for them throughout the year, but the primary effort is to incorporate them into every facet of parish community life. Last but not least, the people give generously to the poor and needy through a local inter-faith food pantry, and Mary's Choice, a foundation founded by Mary Beth Reichart to house and assist needy pregnant women who might other wise have abortions.

Saint Mary Cathedral,
– Colorado Springs –

*T*he development of the Catholic Church in Colorado Springs took place in stages. Pioneer priest Father Joseph Machebeuf celebrated the area's first Mass in 1860 in Old Colorado City. Until the first full-time pastor, Father Frederick Bender, built a worship space in 1877, it was difficult for anyone to feel a sense of community, but a cohesive group of Catholics met regularly in private homes, meeting halls, stores and temporary chapels. Fire destroyed the original structure. The railroad made travel between Denver and Colorado Springs easier for missionary priests. The area had also attracted gold prospectors and miners. The area also developed a reputation for promoting healing because of its hot springs and fresh air, drawing an influx of tuberculosis patients and health care workers.

Devoted Catholics met in the Reading Room of the *Gazette* offices. Unlike larger cities and on the east and west coasts, which were usually identified with particular ethnic groups, Colorado Springs did not have enough people to merit establishing ethnic parishes. All ethnic groups worshiped together. The basement of the present structure was completed by 1891. Religious services have been held on this site continuously for more than a century. St. Mary is the mother church of Roman Catholicism in the Pikes Peak region. By the time parishioners completed this edifice, Catholics had been practicing their faith in Colorado Springs for nearly 25 years. Its superstructure, completed and dedicated in 1898, is architecturally significant. Bell towers were installed in 1902, and a remodeling project that ran from 1902 to 1904 added electric lights, six aisle windows, and arched Gothic ceilings. The original pipe organ was replaced in 1916 and used until 2002.

Parishioners opened a school in 1884 and invited the Sisters of Loretto to teach the girls at what became Loretto Academy. Families that had moved to the city in the first wave of settlers were now seeing their children create a second generation of worshipers, and the community spirit demonstrated itself as early as 1894 during a parish-wide mission to rally those who had fallen away from the church.

Economic problems led to a decline in the school in the 1980s and its closing in 1987. However, some parishioners decided to reopen the high school under private auspices and presently, it remains strong with increasing numbers of parents opting for the values-based Catholic education over public schools.

A downtown parish, St. Mary has long been a place where people in need come for help from its emergency-assistance programs. The parish continues to serve the poor and needy. The Social Concerns ministry works for social justice and coordinates parish activities for direct service, discussion groups, legislative advocacy efforts and community development. Parishioners visit the sick and homebound, comfort the grieving, participate in Respect Life activities and have formed a Stephen Ministry that reaches out to individuals in need with one-on-one connections.

Saint Michael,
– Calhan –

*F*ather G. Raber, then pastor in Elbert, Colorado, erected a small church in Calhan in 1905, the area's first, serving as the main church for missions in Ramah, Matheson, and Holtwood. The church's name honors Michael Balsick, a Catholic pioneer who at the turn of century opened his home for Mass. Between 1905 and 1920, priests from Elbert served the faithful. Two other churches were constructed in 1917 — in Ramah and in Mathson — and then later in Holtwood for its tiny congregation. Father Zybura, who was assigned as a resident pastor in 1920, bought a house that year to be used as a rectory. He oversaw all four missions, comprised of about 55 farming, ranching and small town families, until he fell ill later that year.

The congregation numbered about 60 families for many years. The three other missions consolidated into St. Michael after the construction of its present church in 1964. The last decade has brought an influx of subdivisions and city people, who have contributed to parish dynamics. Welcoming efforts enhance this small faith community.

Without a staff, the parish provides a number of faith-based services, including pastoral council, a men's club, a women's society, a youth group and a choir. Children and adults participate in religious education classes. There is a vacation Bible school. The parish supports ecumenical outreach activities and was instrumental in co-founding the local Ministerial Association with other churches. The association coordinates local charities and temporary facilities for stranded winter travelers. More than 40 percent of the congregation participates in outreach and parish activities besides weekly Mass attendance, and this personal commitment has resulted in a small financial surplus that is tithed to local community needs as much as possible.

*E*stablished in 1981 with Father John Slattery as the founding pastor, St. Patrick originally served about 30 families in the Metro North Region of the diocese. From its inception, the parish has been known as hospitable, caring and giving, committed to tithing and to community service. The parish has grown to more than 2,300 families, counting more than 7,000 individuals, many of whom have committed to the parish's many outreach ministries. They volunteer time and financially support a food pantry, a soup kitchen and a St. Vincent de Paul Society council which operates an emergency services outreach. Parishioners also support a ministry of meals, outreach to the homebound, a health ministry and SHARE Colorado, a self-help and resource-exchange program. In addition they have organized an array of committees, including groups that work for social justice, provide transportation, volunteer with Project Gabriel, comfort and aid the grieving and serve the poor.

St. Patrick offers an array of religious formation programs from preschool through adult, including a vibrant RCIA, a Stephen Ministry and others that foster spiritual growth. An active parish life includes annual events such as Ministry Day, the St. Patrick Day Parade, Mom's Night Out and other celebrations that attract visitors. Volunteers provides nursery and child-care aid.

Parishioners recently constructed a memorial garden where people can remember their loved ones and seek peace, encouragement and comfort 24 hours a day. Boy Scouts erected a gazebo where one can rest. The garden features a large water fountain, surrounded by rose bushes, flowers, blooming shrubs and trees. Parishioners plan to add a statue of Rachel, the matriarch of Israel who mourned for her children and other innocents, to comfort parents who have lost children.

Saint Paul,
– Colorado Springs –

*P*astoral leaders of what is now St. Mary's Cathedral built a chapel — dedicated in 1919 — in the Broadmoor community, an event sparked by a generous donation from Spencer and Julie Penrose. When it attained parish status in 1925, it was designated as St. Paul Catholic Church with Father Louis Hagus appointed as the first pastor. Next to the chapel, parishioners built a rectory that included a parish hall, church offices and priests' residence.

Pauline Memorial Catholic School opened in 1955 with kindergarten through fourth grades. The growing congregation built a larger church in 1959; Christmas Eve Mass in the year of construction was the parish's first Mass in the new structure, which was dedicated in 1960. During the construction phase, the congregation continued to celebrate Mass in the chapel. The following year, the parish built a convent and expanded the school to eight grades. The convent was converted into an administration office and activity center in 1985.

With the help of the Loyola University's Parish Evaluation Project, St. Paul conducted a survey of parish needs in 1997 and determined to make major repairs to its aging facilities. It launched a major building expansion, adding a large hall, conference rooms, a library, youth center, educational resource center, a new gymnasium and a junior high wing.

Parishioners support more than 20 outreach ministries. They collect and distribute food and grocery certificates for several local food pantries. Eucharistic ministers visit the sick and home-bound; several of the parish's scouting youth have earned the Pillars of Faith and the Summit Awards for their service. Parish nurses administer flu shots, and the Knights of Columbus host social activities. The parish sponsors blood drives after Sunday morning Mass and organizes missions to the inner city, all while sustaining its school.

𝒮t. Peter traces its heritage to the early 1900s, when a dozen families celebrated Mass at the Modern Woodmen of the World Hall. The parish, which began as a mission, served Catholics north of El Paso County and in southern Douglas County. Construction of a church began in 1911; this building now stands north of the new church. Although it remained a mission for many years, St. Peter grew along with the area. Sisters from Mount St. Francis formed religious education classes in 1958, and the Women's Guild was organized in 1964. By the early 1970s, the small, white-frame church was too small for the 90 families worshipping there, and the congregation built a new church just south of the original one. The first Mass in this new structure was celebrated in 1978; the church was dedicated in 1979.

The mission attained parish status in 1984 with Father Dean Kumba appointed as the first resident pastor. Under Father Kumba's leadership, the parish grew quickly, and, by the 1990s, had again outgrown its worship space. Construction of a larger church began in 1992. It was completed and dedicated in 1994.

Today, more than 1,500 families make the parish their spiritual home. The religious education program serves more than 700 students of all ages. Bible study classes, Familia and Regnum Christi groups and other activities foster spiritual growth and community service. Parishioners provide aid to the area's needy and support the Marian House soup kitchen with food and clothing donations. They send shoe boxes packed with personal items and gifts to the Pine Ridge Indian Reservation each Christmas and participate in many other outreach activities, including visiting the sick and homebound, providing shelter to stranded motorists and serving the homeless, all to achieve their mission of "commitment through community through Christ."

Saint Rose of Lima,
- Buena Vista -

*W*hen Buena Vista was known as Cottonwood in 1858, Father Joseph Machebeuf oversaw a mission there for 19 years before a church was built. Mass was celebrated in private homes for a small congregation drawn from mining camps. The Denver and Rio Grande Railroad brought rapid growth to Buena Vista in 1880. A Catholic church was constructed in 1881 in the building rush, when street lines and lot surveys were not well observed. Many buildings were constructed on wrong lots or in the streets, the church among them. It was moved to its proper site in 1888. Various diocesan priests and the Benedictine Fathers from Canon City served Buena Vista Catholics until 1956, when the Diocese of Colorado Springs took it over from the Diocese of Santa Fe, New Mexico. The first resident pastor was appointed in 1963.

When parishioners moved into a newly constructed parish complex, dedicated in 1967, they abandoned the original church. A plan for the Buena Vista Volunteer Fire Department to burn the building — one of the region's oldest Catholic churches — caused a controversy in spring 1969. A restraining order halted the action, and it was moved to a Forest Square Park where it now serves as the visitor center and office of the Chamber of Commerce.

Currently, nearly 300 families volunteer in an array of outreach ministries, providing groceries for the elderly and disabled through the parish's free store and contributing to a fund that underwrites vouchers for housing, food and gasoline for needy people who contact the police department. The Knights of Columbus and Legion of Mary serve the community, and an Angel Ministry, formed in 2001, supports and encourages young adults, young couples, college students and military personnel.

*V*ietnamese Holy Martyrs was founded in 1975 when refugees from Communist-controlled Vietnam came to Colorado. Father Minh Than Tran from the United States Council celebrated Mass in a private home for approximately a half a dozen families in 1976. They then celebrated Mass at Pauline Chapel next to St. Paul church in the Broadmoor neighborhood from 1984-92.

The community was named the Vietnamese Holy Martyrs Quasi-Parish in 1992. The name commemorates Vietnamese Christians persecuted in the 19th century. Many of them were tortured when rulers marked the words "ta dao," or "false religion" on them and tried to force them to renounce their faith by trampling a crucifix. The 117 who were canonized in 1988 included 96 Vietnamese, 11 Spanish Dominicans and 10 French members of the Paris Society for Foreign Missions. They suffered beheading and suffocation; some were mutilated and burned alive. They were beatified on four separate occasions between 1900 and 1951.

The parish celebrated Mass in the basement of the old diocesan chancery across the street from St. Mary Cathedral in downtown Colorado Springs from 1992 until acquiring the old Calvary Baptist church in 2001. A statue of the Virgin Mary stands in front of the red brick structure, with Roman columns at the entrance.

Father Minh, who remained the pastor for nearly 30 years, died shortly after his retirement in 2002.

Parishioners at Vietnamese Holy Martyrs sing traditional Catholic hymns with a Vietnamese flair, demonstrating a marriage of the East and the West in their Masses. The parish celebrates its patronal feast day on Nov. 24. Masses continue to be offered in Vietnamese, with hope that an English-language Mass will be added in the future.

Teller Catholic Community

The Teller Catholic Community consists of three churches: one parish and two missions: Our Lady of the Woods in Woodland Park, St. Peter in Cripple Creek and St. Victor in Victor.

Saint Peter,
- Cripple Creek -

St. Peter in Cripple Creek was established in 1892 with a small frame church constructed on the highest hill in town. The congregation grew, and soon a larger church was needed. The first service in the new church took place on Easter Sunday 1898, and the church was dedicated one month later. The parish opened a school, staffed by the Sisters of Mercy, in 1901. On the first day, the Sisters had to turn away more than a 100 students. A second story was added to the school building during 1902; more than 250 children were enrolled that autumn. The fledgling school thrived, serving the community for 25 years.

Saint Victor,
- Victor -

During the 1890s, Victor, a bustling town 2,000 strong, claimed 12 Catholic families. Father Edward Downey was named the first priest to St. Victor in 1894, and the first Mass was celebrated in the Baptist Church. For several months Mass was also offered in a lumber yard office and in a private home until a frame structure was obtained and dedicated in 1895. St. Victor's rapidly increasing Catholic population had grown to more than 20 families, prompting the need for a new, larger church. Free of debt and considered one of the finest structures in the city, the new church was dedicated in 1903, large enough to serve the more than 350 families it now counted. When Victor began to decline after 1917, so did the parish, through the 1920s. In 1928, it became mission of St. Peter. But by the late 1930s, Catholics in Victor outnumbered those in Cripple Creek

and so St. Victor once again — after a decade — had a resident priest, who served both churches.

Since their founding, Cripple Creek and Victor have contended about which was the larger. While St. Victor boasted a larger number of Catholics in the 1930s, by 1943 Corpus Christi in Colorado Springs served both parishes.

Our Lady of the Woods,
- Woodland Park -

*E*stablished in 1954 in Woodland Park with Father Michael Kavanagh as founding pastor, Our Lady of the Woods was designated a mission of St. Peter in Monument and St. Victor in Victor. Mass for its 17 families was celebrated in the Woodland Park gymnasium, at the guest home of a local family and at the VFW building (currently the Woodland Park Senior Citizen Center). Construction of a church began in 1954; it was dedicated in 1955. For several years, parishioners celebrated "Christmas in August" so that summer residents and visitors could see the church with Christmas decorations and assist the church through winter with their offerings. As a result of this celebration, the church was able to retire its debt in 11 years.

Woodland Park grew rapidly while Cripple Creek and Victor declined, and soon Father Kavanagh began serving all Teller County Catholics. St. Peter and St. Victor became missions of Our Lady of the Woods.

The combined faith community considers itself as one family on the same journey. Each church continues to support a small and friendly faith community, but their active combined social ministry helps both parishioners and others with needs such as food, transportation, paying bills, car repairs, home visitation and a variety of services. The community counts more than 300 children in elementary through high school ages and offers a variety of religious education programs to meet their needs. A combined ministry to the homebound, a prayer chain, a prayer group, the oldest council of Knights of Columbus in Colorado and a youth group serve the needy and organize social activities and fundraising events. A number of combined groups foster spiritual growth. Teller County Catholics meet at four locations, including once monthly in Florissant, where they nourish a small, fledgling faith community.

Saint Mary's High School,
- Colorado Springs -

*T*his year marks the 123rd anniversary of continuous operation for St. Mary's High School. With a dedicated faculty, committed parents, and a community of alumni and friends, the school stands as a testimony to Catholic education in Colorado Springs. This effort began in 1885, when the Sisters of Loretto, a teaching order from Nerinkx, Kent., sent three Sisters to found Loretto Academy at the request of Father Robert Byrne, pastor of St. Ann, and Bishop Joseph Machebeuf, bishop of Denver. Sisters Columba Gallavan, Walburta Sullivan and Jovita Mills enrolled nine girls the first semester and 11 more the second, holding classes in a rented house near the city's center. Within a year, the Sisters purchased a premium site in the population center and constructed a four-story brick school with residential facilities for the Sisters on the fourth floor. Enrollment grew rapidly. Boys under age 12 were admitted in 1898.

The school became the city's premier private school. St. Ann purchased the land next to the academy in 1893 and constructed a new church. By the church's completion in 1897, the parish had changed its name to St. Mary's; the Sisters agreed to change the school's name to St. Mary's in 1902, to accept boys through eighth grade and to add a high school for girls. In return, the parish would enlarge the school and assume maintenance costs. Enrollment climbed, and by 1912 the par-

ish wanted more control. The sisters sold the building and all its contents to the parish, agreeing to teach for $25 each per month.

The school thrived, and in 1920 the building was expanded. A young priest, Father (later Monsignor) William Kelly became school superintendent in 1932, leading St. Mary's for 28 years. Under his guidance, athletic teams flourished and state championship banners adorned the gym walls. The school stated elaborate operettas directed by Father Kelly.

Burgeoning enrollment during the post-World War II decade strained the "Ole Green," as the academy building was affectionately called. A new building was constructed across the street for the elementary grades, but as high school enrollment increased, elementary school numbers decreased, and by 1962 the elementary grades were phased out. High school students occupied both buildings.

The Diocese of Denver built a Catholic Education Center on the football practice field next door to the former elementary school. Completed in 1971, the new center housed the high school and diocesan offices, and "Ole Green" was razed on March 31, 1971.

For nearly a century, 233 Sisters of Loretto had served St. Mary, but gradually, their numbers decreased. The last one to leave St. Mary's, in 1985, was Sister Gladys Ann Givan, a grand niece of the first to arrive, Sister Columba Gallavan.

Established in 1984, the Diocese of Colorado Springs oversaw the school's operation but could not sustain its large debt. Bishop Richard Hanifen reluctantly announced that the school would close in 1987.

A dedicated parent group formed a non-profit Committee for Catholic Secondary Education in Colorado Springs. They negotiated with the diocese and reopened St. Mary's as an independent school in the fall of 1987, operating with the approval of the local bishop. After five years of leasing the building from the diocese, the committee purchased a building on Yampa Street and moved the school in the summer of 1992.

Capital campaigns improved the campus over the past decade and a half, and in fall 2006 the Grace Center for Athletics and Community Service opened on a nearby 25-acre parcel. In St. Mary's second century, enrollment continues to climb and some classes have a waiting list, a testimony to the Sisters' legacy of Catholic education.

Benet Hill Monastery

$\mathcal{E}$stablished in 1965, the Benet Hill Monastary is an independent daughter house of Mount St. Scholastica, Atchison, Kan.. The Benedictine Sisters assumed the ministry of educating the poor in Colorado, a ministry begun by the Atchison Sisters in 1913. The Sisters taught in elementary and secondary public schools in Antonito, Capulin and Conejos and in St. Mary, the Catholic school in Walsenburg. They also staffed Catholic elementary schools in Alamosa, Monte Vista, Pueblo, Colorado Springs and Denver. The Atchison Sisters had purchased in 1960 the former San Luis Ranch School for Girls in Colorado Springs and established Benet Hill Academy in 1963. Benet Hill Academy provided more than 680 girls with an education based on academic excellence and Catholic values until 1982.

In response to the needs of the times, the Sisters began making ministry transitions into religious education, special education, vocational rehabilitation, health services — as nurses and as hospital chaplains — and retreat ministry in 1972.

They developed in the 1980s a retreat ministry at the Benet Pines Retreat Center in Black Forest — land originally purchased in 1966 — and emphasized Benedictine hospitality, a serene environment for prayer and reflection and retreat services for groups and individuals. All faith traditions continue to be welcome to discover God more fully through private or directed retreats. Accommodations for overnight guests and for day and group seminars enable anyone to participate in Benedictine community life, including hermitages for those wanting an intense experience of solitude. The grounds offer a variety of unique prayer sites with interconnecting meditative paths, conducive to quiet reflection and contemplation. Echoed in the tranquility are the simple monastic rhythm of Liturgy of the Hours, lectio divina and interaction with the small Benedictine community's peace and tranquility.

Established in 1982, the Center at the monastery continues to offer a wide range of programs in spirituality, Scripture, personal enrichment, art and pastoral services. The Benet Hill Center is now home to Colorado Springs Charter Academy, organized in 2005. The

Academy is not part of the local school district but is one of the two schools accepted by the Colorado Charter School Institute, serves nearly 240 kindergarteners through sixth-graders.

With more than 400 young musicians from the Colorado Springs community traveling and performing worldwide, the Colorado Springs Youth Symphony maintains offices at the Center. Also, numerous groups, businesses, and individuals hold special events, graduations, dance recitals, renewal days, meetings and other activities there.

Dedicated in 1987, Our Lady of Peace Chapel complex remains the focal point of monastic life, where the community gathers thrice daily for Liturgy of the Hours and for Mass.

Since the 1970s, the Sisters have served in a variety of parish and diocesan ministries throughout Colorado and in nearby states, holding leadership positions in human service and educational institutions.

Mission assignments abroad for individual Benet Hill Sisters have included El Salvador, Guyana, Nicaragua and Cuba. Sister Naomi Rosenberger serves in the Diocese of Mandeville, Jamaica.

Currently, 38 sisters comprise the community. Their varied activities demonstrate the heart of their ministry:

to seek God in the monastic community, to praise God in liturgy, to grow in God through contemplation and study, and to serve God by using their gifts and talents in a variety of ministries.

Mount Saint Francis

*L*ocated in the Pikes Peak region of Colorado Springs on 110 acres nestled in the foothills of the Rampart Range of the Colorado Rocky Mountains, Mount St. Francis is home to the St. Joseph Province of the Sisters of St. Francis of Perpetual Adoration. The Sisters use their beautiful grounds, buildings and facilities to provide services, activities and programs designed to enhance the total well-being of individual groups and families. Their motherhouse, also situated on the campus, is the home for the province's formation program, where women discern a vocation to the community and prepare to make their vows. A home to all Sisters of the Province, the Motherhouse also serves as a centerpoint for Sisters ministering in other areas of Colorado and in Nebraska, New Mexico, Texas, and Kentucky.

The Sisters are committed to serving the poor and to promoting quality of life through mercy, justice and compassion. To this end, they partner with others who work for the same goals, including Franciscans International, Amnesty International and Centers of Concern, among others.

The Sisters founded the Franciscan Community Counseling, a private, non-profit agency that aims to improve the quality of life of individuals and families, regardless of their ability to pay. The agency promotes activities to foster wellness and prevent sickness. Its professional staff persons hold advanced degrees in counseling, social work, psychology and marriage and family therapy. Staff members collaborate with others to provide high-quality services in a cost-effective manner and assist clients in maintaining or restoring their emotional, mental, physical and spiritual well-being. The facility operates a site in downtown Colorado Springs in addition to the one at Mount St. Francis.

The Sisters founded a Women Partnering service in 1998 to address the needs of Colorado Springs' women and children. The service, based on research conducted by the Sisters, first identifies unmet needs and then mobilizes the community to help the women develop self-reliance. The Sisters partnered with six vulnerable women from 1990 to 2000 in a research process that focused on building community and shaping the service into an effective tool.

With a tradition that includes over a century of experience in providing health care, the Sisters at Mount St. Francis continue their mission through the Mount St. Francis Nursing Center. The 108-bed facility offers respite, rehabilitation, long-term and hospice care. Residents at the nursing facility can participate in an array of activities and outings, attend daily Mass and other religious services, meet with a chaplain if need be, gather at an ice cream parlor and visit with family members on several outdoor patios.

The Sisters also operate the Franciscan Retreat Center, which consists of three buildings that contain 34 bedrooms with baths, two handicapped-equipped bedrooms, two large conference rooms, three small meeting rooms, a lobby, fireplace and a reception area that accommodates 120 people in a quiet, reflective atmosphere.

The Sisters rely on their God-given talents to respond to the needs within the Church and in society. The Sisters are engaged in the well-established ministries of health care, education, pastoral care, parish ministry, care of the elderly, counseling, social work, religious education and administration. In the last sentence include the following suggestions: "In addressing current human needs, the Sisters minister to elderly poor, the disabled, hospice participants, immigrants, Native American and Hispanic communities and to Catholic parishes."

In the 1980's, the Sisters availed their chapel and two stone buildings to the Diocese of Colorado Springs to accommodate the establishment of St. Francis of Assisi Parish which currently ministers to surrounding neighborhoods.

The Sisters of St. Francis of Perpetual Adoration were founded by Mother Maria Theresia Bonzel in Olpe, Germany on July 20, 1863 and December 14, 1875 marked the arrival of the first Sisters in Lafayette, Indiana. Currently, Provinces are established in Germany, the Philippines, Indiana and Colorado. The Sisters also have a Region in Brazil.

Sources Consulted

- - -

Archives of the Diocese of Colorado Springs
Archives of the Archdiocese of Denver
The Colorado Catholic Herald-Colorado Springs
Pikes Peak Edition-Denver Catholic Register

- - -

Carl Abbot, Stephen J. Leonard, Thomas J. Noel, *Colorado: A History of the Centennial State, 4th ed.*, (Boulder: University Press of Colorado, 2005)

Donna Drucker, *To Your Holy Mountain: The History of St. Mary's Cathedral in Colorado Springs* (Colorado Springs: Star Publications, 1999, 2000)

Thomas J. Noel, *Colorado Catholicism and the Archdiocese of Denver, 1857-1989* (Boulder: University Press of Colorado, 1989)

■ Pioneers Museum